Beginning Object-Oriented ASP.NET 2.0 with VB.NET

From Novice to Professional

Brian R. Myers

Apress®

Beginning Object-Oriented ASP.NET 2.0 with VB.NET: From Novice to Professional

Copyright © 2005 by Brian R. Myers

ISBN (pbk): 1-59059-538-6

Printed and bound in the United States of America 9 8 7 6 5 4 3 2 1

Trademarked names may appear in this book. Rather than use a trademark symbol with every occurrence of a trademarked name, we use the names only in an editorial fashion and to the benefit of the trademark owner, with no intention of infringement of the trademark.

Lead Editor: Jonathan Hassell
Technical Reviewers: Ron Landers, Martin W.P. Reid
Editorial Board: Steve Anglin, Dan Appleman, Ewan Buckingham, Gary Cornell, Tony Davis,
    Jason Gilmore, Jonathan Hassell, Chris Mills, Dominic Shakeshaft, Jim Sumser
Associate Publisher: Grace Wong
Project Manager: Kylie Johnston
Copy Edit Manager: Nicole LeClerc
Copy Editor: Julie M. Smith
Assistant Production Director: Kari Brooks-Copony
Production Editor: Ellie Fountain
Compositor: Linda Weidemann, Wolf Creek Press
Proofreaders: Elizabeth Berry and Linda Seifert
Indexer: Carol Burbo
Artist: Kinetic Publishing Services, LLC
Interior Designer: Van Winkle Design Group
Cover Designer: Kurt Krames
Manufacturing Manager: Tom Debolski

Distributed to the book trade worldwide by Springer-Verlag New York, Inc., 233 Spring Street, 6th Floor, New York, NY 10013. Phone 1-800-SPRINGER, fax 201-348-4505, e-mail orders-ny@springer-sbm.com, or visit http://www.springeronline.com.

For information on translations, please contact Apress directly at 2560 Ninth Street, Suite 219, Berkeley, CA 94710. Phone 510-549-5930, fax 510-549-5939, e-mail info@apress.com, or visit http://www.apress.com.

*This book is dedicated to my dad, Donald Myers Jr.,
who helped me understand the value of work
and who thought I should "do something
in computers." I am very glad I took that advice.*

In Loving Memory of Donald Myers Jr.
February 18, 1945–April 23, 1998

Contents at a Glance

Contents

About the Author

BRIAN MYERS is a software engineer and database administrator for a large manufacturing company. He is a Microsoft Certified Solution Developer for .NET, a Microsoft Certified Application Developer for .NET, and a Microsoft Certified Professional. He holds an Associates Degree in Microcomputer Applications Development from the Pennsylvania College of Technology and a Bachelors of Information Systems from Pennsylvania State University. Along with his professional accreditations, he is also an Eagle Scout.

He has been working with VB since VB 5 and has been writing OOP applications for over seven years. He has more than seven years of experience as a software developer, mostly with Microsoft technologies. Prior to taking his current position in June 2004, he worked for a consulting company for six years, handling various development projects as a developer as well as a project manager.

Brian has also written articles for www.AspToday.com as well as teaching courses in .NET development and SQL Server.

About the Technical Reviewer

RONALD LANDERS is the President and Senior Technical Consultant for IT Professionals, Inc. (ITP), a staffing, recruiting, development, and IT project services company. Mr. Landers has over 20 years of experience in the IT field and specializes in database design and implementation, application design and architecture, and web-based technologies, such as web services, electronic commerce, and web portals.

In addition to ITP, Mr. Landers has been teaching IT classes for UCLA Extension for the past 13 years. Currently, Mr. Landers's courses include beginning and advanced classes in SQL Server, ASP.NET, Web Services, and Object Oriented Programming.

Acknowledgments

First I would like to thank my wife, Catharine Miller, for her support while I wrote this book. Thank you for giving me the time to write this book as well as teach. Thank you for allowing me to do what I love and love what I do. A very big thank you goes to Amy Cook and Jennifer Bitting for reviewing my development drafts, and for giving me feedback. Without your initial feedback, the revision process would have taken much longer. Thank you to Jon Hassell, my editor, for helping me along with my first book. Thank you also to many others at Apress, such as Dominic Shakeshaft for giving me the opportunity to write this book, Kylie Johnston for helping the book along the process, Julie Smith for the copy editing, and Ellie Fountain for helping the book through production. Without the whole team at Apress I would not have been able to write this book.

This book, as well as my career, would not have been started without the help of the instructors at the Pennsylvania College of Technology. The instructors not only taught me software development, but also taught me the value of not just concentrating on technology. The most important of these instructors was not only my instructor but also my advisor, Mr. Al Henry. He helped me see that to be a well-rounded software developer, I also needed to take business courses to understand the business side of any organization. I used that advice to pursue my Bachelors of Information Systems degree from Penn State, which required 50% of its credits in IT-related courses and 50% of its credits in business-related courses. Without Mr. Henry's urging, I probably wouldn't have taken more business courses and I probably would not be where I am today in my professional career. I hope that is a lesson to other young software developers—to compete in the current environment, you must understand business.

Finally I want to thank the rest of my family—my mother Betty, my sister Michelle, and my brother Jim. I am very grateful for everything that you have done for me.

One last thing, to my niece Erica and nephew Ryan: See, this shows you can do anything you want to.

Introduction

This book was born out of a lunch that I had with two colleagues of mine. They both had an extensive background in mainframe development, but they were struggling to understand what OOP was and how they should apply it. During the conversation, I explained some of the basics of OOP and afterwards thought about better ways to teach these developers the concepts of OOP. That lead me to decide that I should write a book, which lead me to Apress—and the rest is history.

Object-Oriented Programming is important in today's ever-changing world. More and more businesses are abandoning mainframe development for client/server development. Client/server development is greatly enhanced by OOP techniques. OOP techniques teach developers to build reusable code and to think about a problem in terms of the real world. OOP is all about modeling the real world to make more user- and business-friendly software applications.

In the past couple of years, Microsoft announced a new version of .NET that was to be delivered in 2005. Visual Basic 2005, Visual Studio 2005, and ASP.NET 2.0 all provide new functionality and great advantages. This book first teaches the concepts of OOP and then uses the newest version of .NET to develop ASP.NET web sites. Many companies are starting to develop most, if not all applications, as web applications. This book helps position the reader to develop web sites with the newest version of .NET and with OOP concepts.

If you have developed web sites with traditional ASP, you will learn how to develop web sites with VB.NET, which is a very big improvement over traditional VBScript and JavaScript.

Who This Book Is For

There are two main groups that this book was written for. The first is the group of procedural developers that have spent many years writing software for mainframes. The transition from procedural programming to OOP can be a difficult one. This book provides a path for that transition, by first explaining OOP concepts and then explaining how to implement those concepts with the latest technologies from Microsoft. This book also includes a chapter (Chapter 1) that introduces Visual Studio and the whole concept of .NET.

The second group this book was written for is the VB6 and traditional ASP developers. Microsoft is strongly encouraging developers to move to .NET. Whether you agree with that strategy or not, looking at the newest technology and learning how to use it to develop new applications may help solve some very difficult problems. As a developer that first learned VB5, and then VB6, and then made the jump to VB.NET, I know it's scary. You are comfortable with the syntax and the concepts. However, as a developer that has made the transition, I can tell you my development is much quicker now and I can deal with much more complex problems. There are several hurdles that you need to overcome, but this book is a very good first step. If you have not worked with OOP with VB6 or ASP, this book also introduces the concepts. If you have used OOP, then this book will help you transition from VB6 to VB 2005. If you have developed web sites with traditional ASP, then this book will help you find the advantages to ASP.NET and show you how to create web sites with the full VB.NET language, instead of the VBScript or JavaScript languages.

How this Book is Structured

- Chapter 1, "An Introduction to .NET and Visual Studio 2005"

  This chapter provides an introduction to the Microsoft .NET strategy, including an introduction to each of the components, such as the common language runtime. This chapter also includes an introduction to Visual Studio 2005, the latest version of the Visual Studio development tools.

- Chapter 2, "Object-Oriented Programming"

  This chapter provides an overview and introduction to Object-Oriented Programming. This chapter starts by explaining what an object is and why it is important. This chapter then briefly introduces the various Object-Oriented Programming concepts, which are covered in more depth in the remaining chapters.

- Chapter 3, "Attributes and Actions"

  This chapter explains the concepts of attributes and actions within the context of Object-Oriented Programming. After providing an introduction and an Object-Oriented Programming background for each of these concepts, the chapter explains how to implement attributes and actions within VB.NET classes.

- Chapter 4, "Encapsulation"

  This chapter explains the concepts of encapsulation and information hiding within the context of Object-Oriented Programming. This chapter also shows you how encapsulation and information hiding is implemented with the Microsoft .NET Framework and how to implement these concepts with VB.NET.

- Chapter 5, "Inheritance"

  This chapter explains the concept of inheritance within the context of Object-Oriented Programming. This chapter also shows how to implement inheritance within VB.NET. Along with inheritance, this chapter also covers the concepts of overriding and abstract classes. Finally, this chapter shows you how to implement overriding and abstract classes.

- Chapter 6, "Namespaces"

  This chapter covers the concept of a namespace and discusses how namespaces are implemented with the .NET Framework. This chapter starts by covering the purpose of a namespace and then moves into how namespaces are used within the .NET Framework Class Library. Finally, this chapter shows how to implement a namespace and nested namespaces within VB.NET.

- Chapter 7, "Class Design"

  This chapter begins by providing a list of steps for designing a class. The second part of this chapter explains how to implement these steps while designing classes for a Help Desk application. Finally, this chapter shows you how to build the necessary classes within VB.NET for an ASP.NET application, based on the Help Desk application business process presented within this chapter.

- Chapter 8, "ASP.NET Web Forms"

  This chapter shows you how to use the Visual Studio 2005 development environment along with VB.NET to create ASP.NET web pages and web sites. This chapter explains how web forms are processed and discusses the application and session objects. Finally this chapter continues the Help Desk ASP.NET web site begun in Chapter 7 by showing how to build the necessary web pages.

- Chapter 9, "ASP.NET Controls"

This chapter explains the different types of controls that can be used within ASP.NET web sites and how to work with these controls. The chapter also covers the use of master pages within Visual Studio 2005. Finally, this chapter adds new controls to the ASP.NET pages created in the previous chapter for the help desk application.

- Chapter 10, "Web Services"

This chapter covers the basics of web services. This chapter shows you how to create a web service as well as consume a web service with VB.NET. Finally, this chapter shows how to integrate web services with the Help Desk application created in previous chapters.

Prerequisites

- Microsoft Visual Studio 2005

This book uses Visual Studio 2005 Standard Edition. You can also use any other version including Express.

- Microsoft .NET Framework 2.0

Contacting the Author

The author can be reached at bmyersbook@hotmail.com.

■■■

CHAPTER 1

An Introduction to .NET and Visual Studio 2005

This chapter defines VB.NET and ASP.NET and introduces Microsoft .NET and Visual Studio 2005.

VB.NET and ASP.NET

What is an ASP.NET application and what is VB.NET?

The journey towards writing an ASP.NET application with VB.NET begins with understanding those fundamental questions. First of all, some definitions: ASP.NET stands for Active Server Pages .NET, and VB.NET stands for Visual Basic.NET. VB.NET, put simply, is a programming language, and ASP.NET is a technology used to render dynamic web content. An ASP.NET web site is typically made up of code written in either VB.NET or C# (C Sharp). When creating a web site with VB.NET, you are actually creating an ASP.NET application *using* VB.NET. This is different from a traditional Active Server Page (ASP) page, in that an ASP.NET application is written using fully-featured programming languages with full functionality, like VB.NET, instead of scripting languages like Visual Basic Script (VBScript).

An Introduction to Microsoft .NET

Microsoft .NET is a package of software that consists of clients, servers, and development tools. This package includes the Microsoft .NET Framework (to be discussed later), development tools such as Visual Studio 2005 (VS2005), a set of server applications such as Microsoft Windows Server 2003 and Microsoft SQL Server, and client-side applications such as Windows XP and Microsoft Office.

An important piece of the .NET puzzle is the Microsoft .NET Framework, the basis for much of the development part of the .NET strategy. The framework includes many other subcomponents that allow software that has been written in different languages to work together by establishing rules for language independence. Using the Microsoft .NET Framework as a base, software development toolmakers can create development tools for different languages such as COBOL or C++. Microsoft itself used the .NET Framework to create VS, which is a development tool used to create software using the VB or C# programming languages.

The Microsoft .NET Framework also provides many common functions that previously needed to be built by the developer. This includes access to the file system, access to the registry, and easier development when using the Windows Application Programming Interfaces (API) to access operating system–level functionality. This allows the developer to concentrate more on business problems, instead of worrying how to access low-level Windows functionality.

The Common Language Runtime

The Microsoft Common Language Runtime (CLR) is one of the components within the .NET Framework. The CLR provides runtime services, including loading and execution of code. The CLR essentially takes the language-specific code that was written and translates it into what is called Microsoft Intermediate Language (MSIL) code. The resulting code is the same no matter what language the original code was written in. This is what allows code written with VB to work with code written in C#. This is also the most important aspect of the .NET Framework for a software development company, because one developer can write code in VB and another developer can write code with C#, but the application will still work without a problem, allowing companies to use their existing skill sets. Without this framework and the MSIL, an entire application would need to be built using the same language. This would require a software development company to have a full staff of developers that know a specific development language, such as VB.

A single program, written in multiple languages, works mainly because the framework contains a set of common data types that must be used by all languages building applications with the .NET Framework. This set of data types is the Common Type System (CTS), which defines how types are declared, used, and managed. To accommodate the CLR, some of the data types within languages such as VB needed to be changed so they could work better with data types from other languages such as C++. Therefore, if you are a developer who last used a pre-.NET version of Microsoft languages, you may notice various changes within the language, which were necessary since the CLR defines and uses certain rules that must be adhered to by each of the languages that use the .NET Framework.

There is much more to learn about the .NET Framework and the CLR, but, for now, this introduction should lay the groundwork that you will need to begin your first software development with VB.NET. If you'd like more information, there are a vast number of books published on the .NET Framework and on VB and other languages. The Microsoft web site also has a collection of introductory articles and papers within the MSDN .NET Framework Developer Center. The ASP.NET Developer Center can be found at http://msdn.microsoft.com/ASP.NET, and the VS2005 Developer Center can be found at http://lab.msdn.microsoft.com/VS2005 at the time of this writing.

Assemblies

An *assembly* is the main component of a .NET Framework application and is a collection of all of the functionality for the particular application. The assembly is created as either a .dll file for web sites or an .exe file for Windows applications, and it contains all of the MSIL code to be used by the framework. Without the assembly there is no application. The creation of an assembly is automatically performed by VS2005. It is possible to create applications for the .NET Framework without VS—however, you need to use the various tools that come with the .NET Framework Software Development Kit (SDK) to create the assemblies and perform other tasks that are automatically done by VS. Since this is a beginning book, I will not address those other tasks or how to create an assembly without VS.

An Introduction to Visual Studio 2005

VS2005 is the latest version of the Microsoft development tools built to extend and use the .NET Framework. VS2005 is a suite of tools used for developing and designing software using the .NET Framework. There have been two previous versions of VS for .NET—this version adds some new features and continues to make the tools easier to use.

With this version of VS, new ways to purchase and use the tools were presented. Beginning with this version of VS, Microsoft introduced "Express" versions of each Microsoft language tool. For example, you can purchase, install, and use Microsoft Visual Basic Express Edition to write software with VB.NET. There is an advantage to using an Express Edition if you are only developing software with one language such as VB.NET. In that case, you only need to purchase that edition. This decreases the cost of the tools and decreases the amount of space used on your development computer. Also, the Express Editions are fully compatible with the other VS products (such as Standard Edition), so any project built in an Express Edition will work in any of the other editions. The Web Developer Express Edition allows you to create web applications (ASP.NET applications) with either VB.NET or C#. There are two disadvantages to using the Express Editions, however. The first is the inverse of the advantage—with the exception of the Web Developer Edition, you can only create applications with one language when using an Express Edition. For example, only VB.NET applications can be created with the VB.NET Express Edition. The second disadvantage is that the feature set for the Express Edition is more limited than for the Professional or Standard Edition. This version of VS also provides a Team System Edition of VS, which allows software architects and developers to work side by side with the same tools, while they architect, design, and develop software applications. VS Standard Edition is the one covered in this book.

How to Get Started with Visual Studio 2005

The first step in getting started with VS2005 is to choose which version you want to use. There are really two factors to consider when you're deciding which version you want to purchase: the first and most important factor is the breadth of what you plan to do. If you only plan to write Windows applications with VB.NET, then you can use the VB.NET Express Edition. The same holds true if you want to only create C# Windows applications—in that case, you can use the C# Express Edition. If you want to write web applications using only Visual Basic.NET or C#, then you need the Web Developer Express Edition. However, if you want to create both Windows applications and web applications, then you will need one of the full versions of VS.

There are three versions of VS. The difference among them is the functionality each provides. The version with the least amount of functionality is the Standard version. This version does not support remote debugging or SQL Server Reporting Services, and does not include integration with SQL Server 2005. The second version is the Professional version, which includes the features not included in the Standard version. The third and final version is the Team System version. The Team System version includes tools for the entire project lifecycle, including tools for the architect, developer, and tester. The Team System is broken down into components (Team Architect, Team Developer, Team Test, and Team Foundation), which can be installed independently of one another or all together.

The second factor in your decision will most likely be the price. Although this might be the first factor for you, it really shouldn't be—you should buy the edition that suits your needs. The Express Editions will cost the least, followed by the Standard Edition, Professional Edition, and finally the Team System version. If you want to create both Windows applications and web sites, I suggest using the VS Standard, as I do in this book. If you want to only create Windows applications, then the VB.NET or C# Express Edition will provide the necessary functionality. If you want to only create web sites, then the Web Developer Express Edition will provide the necessary functionality. Unless you are working with a large team and within a large organization, the Team System is not necessary for the everyday development of applications.

Once you've identified the version of VS you need, next verify that your system meets the minimum hardware requirements. These requirements are shown in Table 1-1.

Table 1-1. *Minimum Hardware Requirements for VS2005*

Item	Requirement
Processor	Minimum: 600 megahertz (MHz) Pentium, Itanium, Athlon, or Opteron processor Recommended: 1 gigahertz (GHz) Pentium, Itanium, Athlon, or Opteron processor
Operating System	Microsoft Windows 2003 Server Windows XP Professional Windows XP Home Windows 2000 For 64-bit machine, Windows Server 2003 X64 Edition (Build 1184 or later) Windows XP Professional X64 Edition (Build 1184 or later)
RAM	Minimum: 128 MB Recommended: 256 MB
Hard Disk	Without MSDN: 1 GB of available space on system drive 2.5 GB of available space required on installation drive With MSDN: 1.5 GB of available space on system drive 4.5 GB of available space on installation drive
CD or DVD Drive	Required
Display	Minimum: 800 × 600 256 Colors Recommended: 1024 × 786 High Color – 16 bit
Mouse	Microsoft mouse or compatible pointing device

Finally, decide whether you want to create web sites (ASP.NET applications) as well as regular Windows applications. To create web sites, you must first have a web server installed, which is simply software that will take requests for specific web pages and send them to a client, such as Internet Explorer. With VS2005 you have a choice of either installing Internet Information Server (IIS), which is a full blown, industrial strength web server, or using the built in "personal" web server that is automatically installed with VS. The web server that is installed with VS will only serve pages to the local computer, so another computer could not request a page from the web server. This is suitable for development and unit testing.

IIS can be installed and run on Windows 2000 Professional, Windows Server 2003, and Windows XP Professional.

■**Caution** IIS cannot be installed on Windows XP Home Edition.

■**Note** For the rest of this section, I'll assume you have VS2005, Standard Edition installed and ready for use.

Creating a New Web Project (ASP.NET)

After opening VS2005, click File ➤ New ➤ Web Site to create a new web site, as shown in Figure 1-1.

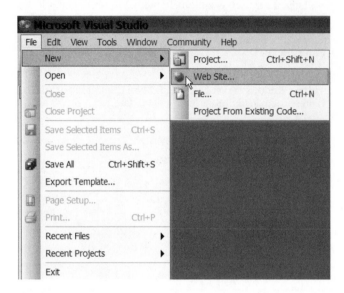

Figure 1-1. *Creating a new web site from the File menu*

Choose ASP.NET Web Site, as shown in Figure 1-2. This will create an ASP.NET web site using VB.NET.

After choosing a type of web site, you will have two choices for the location. You can either create a local IIS web site or a file system web site. To create a local IIS web site, you must first have IIS installed and running. If you are using Windows XP Home Edition, you are not an administrator, or you did not install Internet Information Service, you cannot create a local IIS web site—so skip to the section on creating a file system web site.

Figure 1-2. *Choosing ASP.NET Web Site*

Creating a Local IIS Web Site

To create a web site using IIS, click the Browse button on the New Web Site screen, then click the Local IIS tab in the Choose Location dialog box. This is shown in Figure 1-3.

Click Default Web Site and then click the Create New Web Application button in the top right, as shown in Figure 1-4.

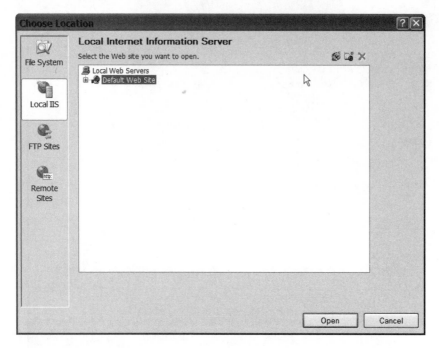

Figure 1-3. *Choosing Local IIS as the web site location*

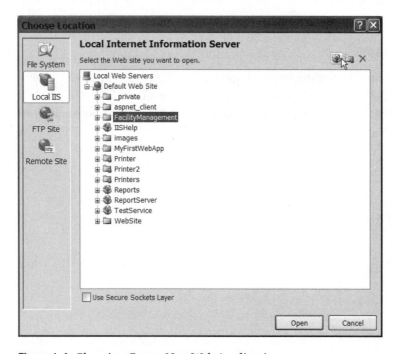

Figure 1-4. *Choosing Create New Web Application*

Type the name of the web site, as you see in Figure 1-5. This is the name that will be used to access the web site within the web server. In this example, `localhost` would be the web server name. The reason `localhost` is the web server name is that it is the web server running on the development computer. If the web site was on another server or was a domain name like Apress.com, the address would be `http://www.apress.com/` followed by the web site name. In this example, I am going to use `localhost` as the address, and I'll name the web site MyFirstWebApp, so the final URL will be `http://localhost/MyFirstWebApp`.

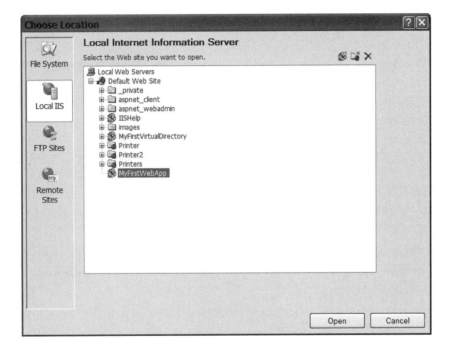

Figure 1-5. *Setting the web site name*

After adding the name, click Open. You will be back to the New Web Site screen with the URL of the application in the location box.

Click OK to create the web site. The first default page will be created.

Creating a File System Web Site

To create a file system web site, which can be used either without IIS installed or to hold the web site files in a directory other than the default for IIS, click the Browse button on the New Web Site screen. Then, click the File System button at the top left, as shown in Figure 1-6.

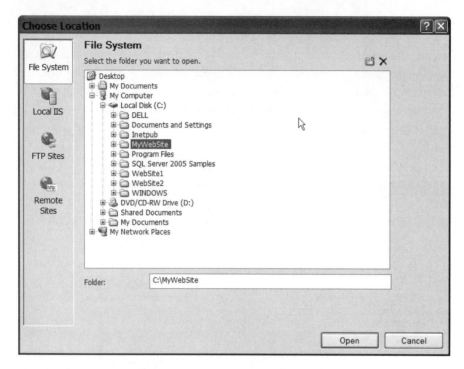

Figure 1-6. *Choosing File System as the Web Site Location*

Choose the folder within the file system that you want to store the files in, and then click Open. Finally, back on the New Web Site screen, click OK. This will create the new project and the default first page.

Project Files

After creating a new project, you will notice there is a file within the Solution Explorer called Default.aspx, with a plus sign (+) beside it. Click the plus sign to expand the Default.aspx.vb file. You can see an example of this in Figure 1-7.

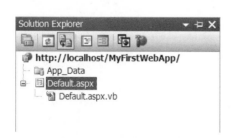

Figure 1-7. *Expanded Solution Explorer with Default.aspx and Default.aspx.vb*

The App_Data folder shown in Figure 1-7 is automatically created when a new web site project is created. This folder can hold Microsoft Access database files, SQL Server Express data files, or XML files.

The difference between Default.aspx and Default.aspx.vb is that the Default.aspx file is used for the presentation of your web site—this could be called the user interface (UI). The Default.aspx.vb file contains all of the actual VB source code that you write for the application, and is called the code file. In traditional Active Server Pages, both the presentation code (HTML tags) and the programming logic (usually VBScript) were in the same ASP file, which made for a rather awkward working environment. Attempting to debug an ASP page with both user interface code (HTML) and logic code (VBScript) could become very difficult to follow. Using the new method, two different developers could potentially work on the same page at the same time—one working on the presentation layer and one in the code file writing the logic that makes the page work. Within VS2005, code files are only defined as partial classes. A partial class is the same structure as a normal class; however, with the keyword partial, VS2005 knows to combine this class with any other partial classes with the same name to create one class when the web site is compiled. This means that multiple developers could be working on the same code file as a partial class. When the whole web site is compiled, the partial classes will all be combined into one.

Working with Virtual Directories

If you have IIS installed you can make a virtual directory from the file system folder that you just created with the IIS Administration Tool. There are two advantages to making a virtual directory instead of just having the folder with files in it. The first is that the virtual directory can be accessed more easily. You can type the web site name that points to the virtual directory (i.e., `http://localhost/MyFirstWeApp`) instead of having to type the URL for a specific web page. The second advantage is that the virtual directory allows you to have the contents of your web site in a different physical location. A virtual directory creates a web site within the default web site and can be accessed using a URL—however, the files that make up the web site are outside of the default location. By default, when IIS is installed, a folder called inetpub is created on the C drive. Typically web site folders are created as subfolders to the wwwroot folder within the inetpub folder. If you are creating a local IIS web site with VS2005, the actual files will be located within the following directory: c:\inetpub\wwwroot\web_site_name. However, with a virtual directory you could have the folder containing the content on another drive. This helps to move more files off the root drive.

To create a virtual directory, open the control panel, then click Administrative Tools (click Performance and Maintenance first if you are using Windows XP). Once the Administrative Tools are open, select Internet Information Services. If you do not see Internet Information Services within the Administrative Tools, IIS is not installed and you cannot create a virtual directory.

After opening Internet Information Services, find your computer's name, choose Web Sites, and then expand the Default Web Site.

Create a new Virtual Directory by first right-clicking Default Web Site and then choosing New ➤ Virtual Directory, as shown in Figure 1-8.

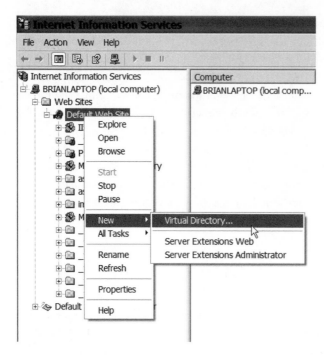

Figure 1-8. *Creating a new Virtual Directory*

Click Next on the opening splash window, then type the *alias* that you want to use. The alias is what the web site will be called. In the previous example, when you created a local IIS web site, the web site was called MyFirstWebApp. That would be the alias of the virtual directory. Enter MyFirstVirtualDirectory as the alias, as shown in Figure 1-9, then click Next.

When you're asked for the directory, click the Browse button and browse to the folder that was created when the File System web site was created earlier, as shown in Figure 1-10.

Click OK on the Browse For Folder pop-up window. Then, click Next on the Directory window. Accept the defaults for the Access Permissions window and then click Next. This will allow read access as well as execution of ASP and ASPX pages. This is enough security for the web site.

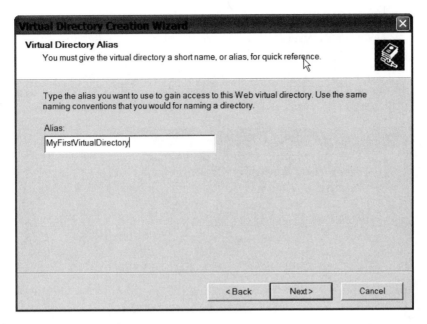

Figure 1-9. *Entering the Virtual Directory alias*

Figure 1-10. *Choosing the folder containing the web site pages*

This security setup will allow users to read from the web site and execute the code on an ASP or ASPX page. However, the user will not be able to write to the folder and therefore will not be able to send malicious code via file to the web site. Finally, you should see a window, as shown in Figure 1-11, saying that the Virtual Directory was created successfully. Click Finish when this window appears.

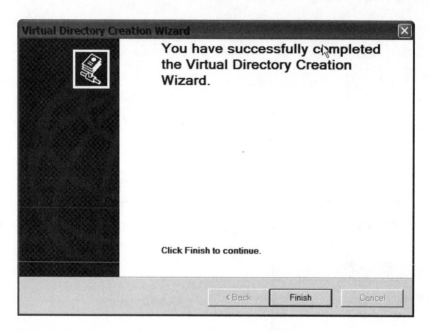

Figure 1-11. *The Virtual Directory has been created.*

If the web site you are creating is for internal use only and all your users are part of the same domain, you can use Windows Authentication to perform the authentication for the web site. By default, both Windows Authentication (called Integrated Windows Authentication) and Anonymous Access are enabled.

To view the Directory Security for the web site, right-click the Virtual Directory you just created and choose Properties. This is shown in Figure 1-12.

Click the Directory Security tab (shown in Figure 1-13) at the top of the Properties window.

Figure 1-12. *Virtual Directory properties*

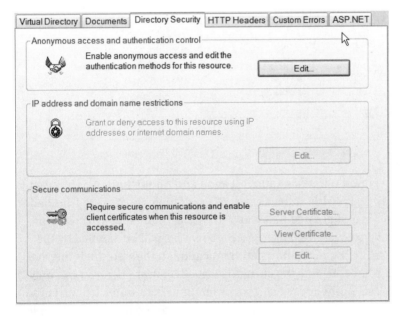

Figure 1-13. *Choosing the Directory Security tab*

Within the Directory Security tab, click the Edit button. The Authentication Methods screen, shown in Figure 1-14, will appear.

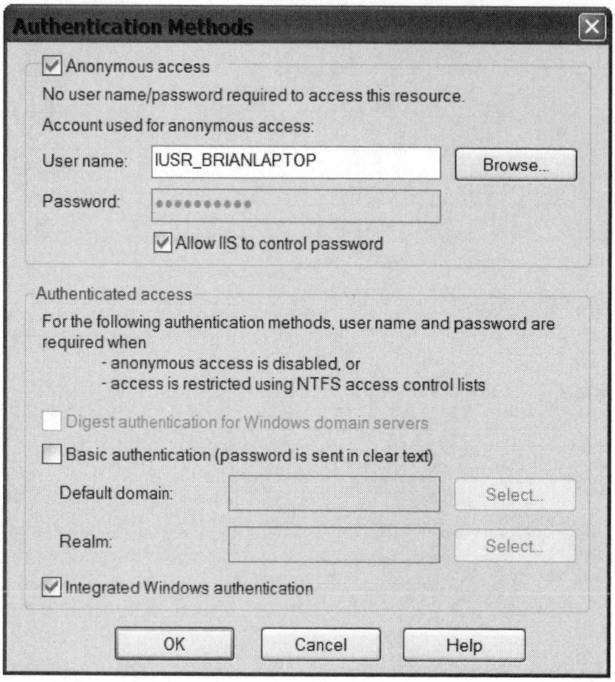

Figure 1-14. *Authentication methods*

Allowing both Integrated Windows Authentication and Anonymous Access permits users to log on to the web site without being part of the domain. If your application is an intranet application, it is suggested that you remove the Anonymous Access. However, if this is an external web site, and username credentials will be handled by the web site, then unselect Integrated Windows Authentication. If the web site is internal and you are attempting to determine the currently logged on user, then you can only select Integrated Windows Authentication. If you attempt to determine the currently logged on user and the web site allows Anonymous Access, your code will not be able to determine the logged on user.

Opening an Existing Web Site

There are two ways to open an existing web site from the File menu. If this is a recent web site (the last four or five projects you worked on), you can click Recent Projects to see a list. The Recent Projects menu option is shown in Figure 1-15.

The other option is to choose Open ➤ Web Site from the File menu, as shown in Figure 1-16.

Make a choice from the options on the left, depending on the type of web site that was created (File System, Local IIS). Then choose the folder the project file is in and click Open, as shown in Figure 1-17.

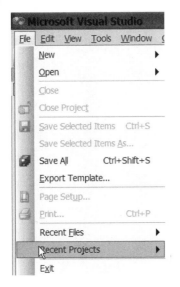

Figure 1-15. *Recent Projects from the File menu*

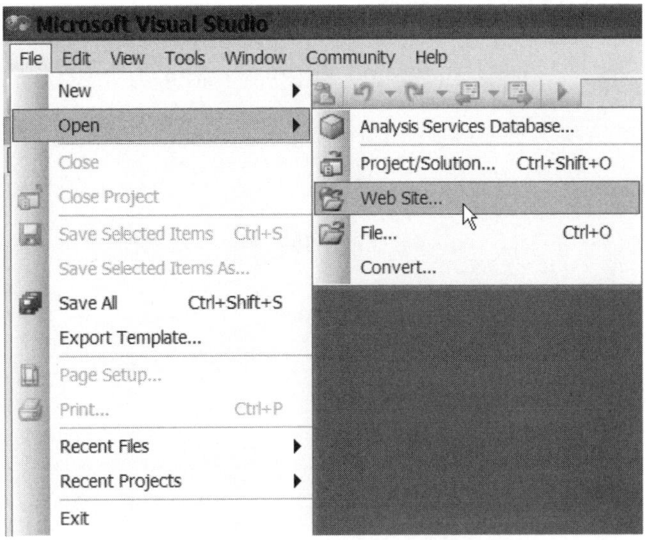

Figure 1-16. *Open ➤ Web Site option from the File menu*

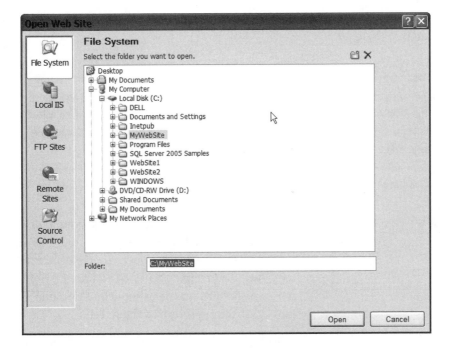

Figure 1-17. *Choosing the folder with the project to open*

Building Web Sites

After opening a web site, the source code file will most likely be showing. Enter **My First Web App** between the HTML tags that say <title>. The source code file with the correct title is shown in Figure 1-18.

```
 1  <%@ Page Language="VB" AutoEventWireup="fals
 2
 3  <!DOCTYPE html PUBLIC "-//W3C//DTD XHTML 1.1
 4
 5  <html xmlns="http://www.w3.org/1999/xhtml" >
 6  <head runat="server">
 7      <title>My First Web App</title>
 8  </head>
 9  <body>
10      <form id="form1" runat="server">
11      <div>
12
13      </div>
14      </form>
15  </body>
16  </html>
17
```

Figure 1-18. *Visual Web Designer*

■**Note** If you do not see a source code page similar to Figure 1-18, then click the View menu and select Solution Explorer. The Solution Explorer will appear. Double-click the file named Default.aspx, which will open a page in the middle section. Then click the source button at the bottom of the middle section to see the HTML source as in Figure 1-18.

Figure 1-19. *Build Web Site menu*

The source code that is showing is HTML. If you click Design at the bottom of the window, this will take you to the Designer tool that you will use later to add elements to the user interface, such as text boxes. From the menu at the top, choose Build ➤ Build Web Site, as shown in Figure 1-19.

The Output window, shown in Figure 1-20, should appear at the bottom of the screen and give the build's status (whether succeeded or failed). If the build failed, a message will appear and a list of the errors will appear for you to correct.

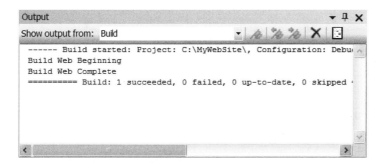

Figure 1-20. *Build Output Window*

Accessing a Web Site

After you build the web site, it's time to test it. If you do not have Internet Information Services installed, hold down Control and press F5. This will start the application. VS will automatically use the VS web server to run the web site. You can also use the Debug menu to debug the web site (see also the "Debugging" section later in this chapter), and VS will use the VS web server if you do not have Internet Information Services installed.

■**Caution** Your anti-virus software may alert you to a problem when first running the web site from within the VS environment. You may need to let your Anti-Virus software know that the VS web server is allowed to process requests.

If you do have Internet Information Services installed, your web site can be accessed in several ways. One way is to open the web site within the Visual Web Developer tool. When the build is completed, an output window should appear at the bottom of the screen, or you will see at least an output tab that you can click on. You may need to scroll up within the Output window to see the link to the web site that was just built. To go to the web site that was just built, hold down the Control key and click the link to the web site in the Output window, as shown in Figure 1-21.

In the previous example, your window within the Visual Web Developer tool should look like Figure 1-22.

Figure 1-21. *The Web Application's link within the Output window*

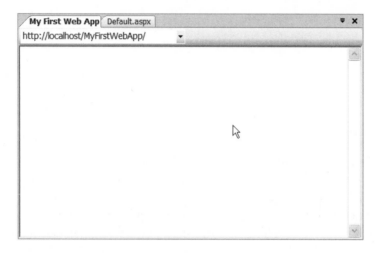

Figure 1-22. *My First Web App running*

The second way to access the web site is to open your Web browser and type the URL. The URL will begin with `http://localhost/` (or the name of the server, if you are working remotely) followed by the web site name. In the examples used so far, the URL will be `http://localhost/MyFirstWebApp`. Typing this URL should bring up the Default.aspx page with the title of My First Web App.

If you change the name of the first page in your web site from Default.aspx, you must change the first document the web server will look for. To do this, open Internet Information Services from the Administrative Tools. Right-click the web site you are working on.

Choose Properties to view the properties of the web site. The Documents tab will appear. The Documents tab is shown in Figure 1-23.

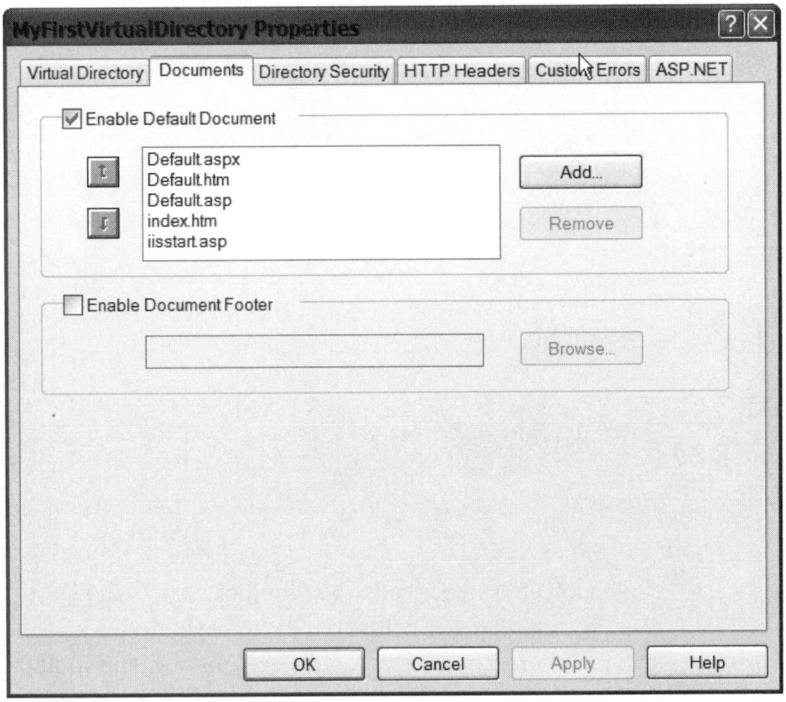

Figure 1-23. *Documents properties tab*

If the name of your first web page within the web site is not in the list, add it by click-ing the Add button and then typing the name of the page, including the extension (for example, .aspx). Then click OK in the pop-up window, click on the name of the file you just added, and then click the up arrow to move it to the top of the list. After moving your page to the top of the list, click OK.

Navigating the Visual Studio Environment

The VS environment can be intimidating at first. However, after you become familiar with it, you can close many of the windows to give yourself more space to work.

The middle section is for coding and includes the Designer Tool. The Designer Tool has two views. The first is the Design view, which is blank when a new form is created. That is where you place controls on the form. The Source view allows you to see the HTML code that makes up the form and is shown in Figure 1-24.

Figure 1-24. *Visual Designer Window*

Figure 1-25.
The Toolbox

The left side area is called the Toolbox, shown in Figure 1-25. This has all of the controls that can be added to a form. To add a control to a form, drag the control from the Toolbox onto the form. There will be more information about creating and working with web forms and web controls in Chapters 8 and 9.

On the right side of the screen there are two boxes; one is the Solution Explorer and the other is the Properties Window. The Solution Explorer, which shows all of the files that are part of the current web site, is shown in Figure 1-26. Use this area to move from page to page while working on the code.

The Server Explorer, shown in Figure 1-27, shows other servers that you have connections to and can be used to connect to and view SQL Server database information. To do this, click on the Data Connections button. Connecting to a database is beyond the scope of this book.

The items shown in the Properties Window, shown in Figure 1-28, will be different depending on the control selected. When you click on any control, or the form itself, information about that control or form will appear in the Properties Window. Use these properties to control all of the visual parts of the controls, such as font and size.

There are two ways you can hide any or all of the windows on the right side of the Properties Window. The first way you can hide a window is by clicking the X in the upper-right

Figure 1-26. *The Solution Explorer*

Figure 1-27. *The Server Explorer*

corner of any of the boxes, closing it completely. The second way is to click the icon that looks like a pushpin in the upper-right corner of each box. If the pushpin is in a downward position, then the window will stay expanded. If the pushpin is in a sideways position, the window will collapse to the side of the screen when not in use. To toggle between the two, click the pushpin. Also, if you have clicked the pushpin to make it collapse the window, and you want to work with the window again, just move your mouse over to the title of the window on the right of the screen and the window will expand again.

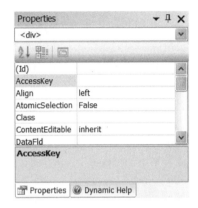

Figure 1-28. *Properties Window*

Debugging

Debugging is an important step in the software development process. Typical industry best practices state that code should be written and then unit tested before integrated with existing code. Unit testing consists of testing the section of code just written with minimal integration into other code that may already exist. Using this strategy means that if an error occurs, there is a limited amount of code that could be responsible for the error.

To best test code and find problems, VS2005, like previous versions, has a debugger included. The debugger allows you to look at each line of code as it is executed and also see the values that a variable contains during execution. The debugger follows the line-by-line execution of the application as if it were in production. This way you know exactly which lines of code will be executed and in what order.

Before using the debugger, a breakpoint must be set. The breakpoint tells the debugger where to stop code execution and begin debugging. Without the breakpoint, the debugger will execute all of the lines of code without showing the debug process.

To see how this works, you are going to add some code to the Default.aspx.vb code file page. Open the Default.aspx.vb page from within the Solution Explorer. If you are in the source code view (meaning you can see the HTML tags), click the Design button at the bottom. Once you are in design mode, right-click and choose View Code. You can right-click anywhere on the page. This will take you to the code page. For now ignore the partial class and inherits lines that are present. These will be covered later. Choose _Default from the top left drop-down menu and use the right drop-down box at the top of the page to choose New, as shown in Figure 1-29.

Figure 1-29. *Choosing New from the right drop-down menu*

Some new lines of code will be added. After the line `Public Sub New()` enter the following lines of code:

```
Dim x as integer
While x<100
X = x + 1
End While
```

These few lines of code will add 1 to x until x is 100. Now, click the gray area just to the left of the code `While x < 100` (see Figure 1-30). This will establish the breakpoint.

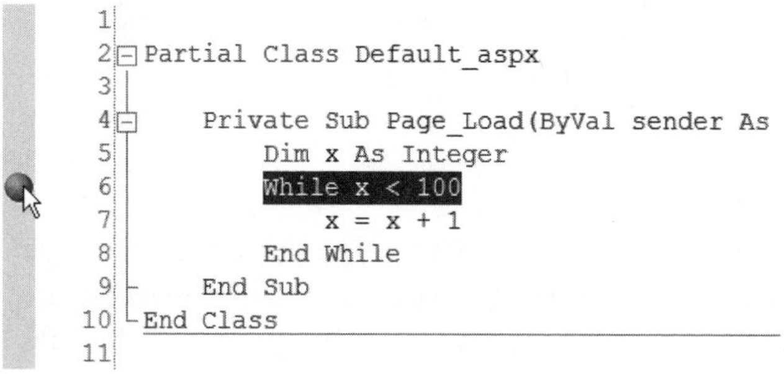

```
 1
 2 Partial Class Default_aspx
 3
 4       Private Sub Page_Load(ByVal sender As
 5            Dim x As Integer
 6            While x < 100
 7                x = x + 1
 8            End While
 9       End Sub
10 End Class
11
```

Figure 1-30. *Add Debugger Breakpoint*

To use the debugger, click the Debug menu and then choose Start. The first time you attempt to debug a new web site you will get a message box, similar to the one shown in Figure 1-31, which will explain that debugging is not enabled for the project by default. There is a web configuration file for each application that you can use. The configuration file can contain information about the project and how the application should behave. Working with the configuration file is outside the scope of this book. For now, click the OK button and the debugger will build the application and begin to debug.

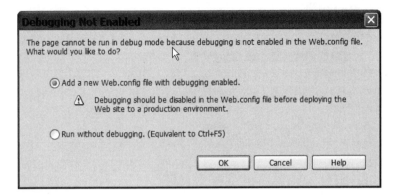

Figure 1-31. *Setting up the configuration file to allow debugging*

First your web browser will open and the page will begin to load. Next, the debug window will appear with a yellow line where the breakpoint is. To move to the next line of code press the F11 key. Continue to press the F11 key to execute the current line of code and then move to the next line. After hitting the F11 key several times, place the mouse over the x in line 7 (either x will do) to get its value at that time. To stop the debugging, either click the Debug menu, then Stop Debugging, or close the web browser window, which will automatically stop the debugging session. You'll use the debugger more in the next few chapters in order to find out what code is executing when and what that particular code is doing.

IntelliSense

IntelliSense is a technology within VS (available for any language within VS) that helps to complete your code. I'll show you an example next. While you still have the web site open, remove line 5 (Dim x as integer). While still on line 5 type **Dim x as** then hit the spacebar. What you should see is a drop-down list that appears after the space that was added after "as." This drop-down gives you a list of all of the possible "things" that x can be created as. In this case, we are going to create x as an integer. When you type an **I**, the drop-down list will automatically move to the first item beginning with I. Type **nte** after the I so you have **Inte**. The drop-down list will stop on Integer, as shown in Figure 1-32. Press the spacebar, and it will finish the word for you. IntelliSense can be very important for working with classes within VB.NET. This will be covered in future chapters.

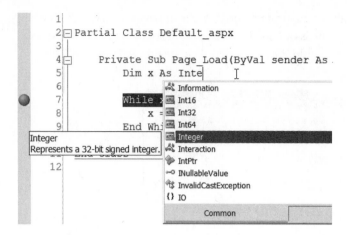

Figure 1-32. *IntelliSense*

Conclusion

In this chapter I have provided you with an introduction to .NET and VS.NET and an explanation of what .NET and the .NET Framework are. I also explained how VS.NET is used to develop applications that work with the .NET Framework. The next chapters will introduce the concepts of object-oriented programming and show how those concepts can be used to build applications with VS.NET and the .NET Framework.

CHAPTER 2

▪▪▪

Object-Oriented Programming

The concepts of object-oriented programming, also known as OOP, are the basis for many of today's programming languages. The languages supported by the .NET Framework and VS are no different. In fact, the .NET Framework is built completely around the concepts of OOP. For you to be able to develop software with VS and specifically VB, you must understand the basic concepts of OOP. In this chapter I'll provide an introduction to OOP concepts and also present an introduction to the use of OOP concepts within VB .NET.

Introduction to OOP Concepts

The core idea within OOP is the concept of an object. An *object* within OOP is something that models a real world entity. An example that I often give is that of a car object. In this case, a car object could represent a real-world car. A car object within the context of OOP would have the same characteristics as a real-world car and would also have the ability to perform actions as a real-world car could. More discussion of the purpose of an object and how objects can be used will follow in the next several sections.

Most real-world objects have *actions* that can be taken either on the objects themselves or by them. In our car object example, starting the car would be an action. To truly model the real world, an object must have or perform actions that the corresponding real-world object would. With the car example, the car object would have an associated action called "start." It may also have an action called "drive" and another called "stop." Most real-world objects also have *attributes* that describe the object. For example, an attribute of a car might be its red color or its size. Attributes can either be changeable or static. The color of a car can be changed, hence color is a changeable attribute, but the size of the car will always remain the same, making the attribute static. Both actions and attributes will be discussed in more detail in Chapter 3.

In the real world, if we are using an object such as a car, we don't need to know the actual inner workings of the car in order to get the benefits of allowing us to move from place to place. In the same way, a key advantage of OOP is the ability to use objects created by other people without having to know how the object actually performs the requested actions. There may be a thousand lines of code within an object that you use daily, but you'll never be exposed to it or need to understand how it works in the course of development. You will only need to know two things:

- Any information you might need to provide to the object

- The kinds of information you will get out of the object

This is a concept called *encapsulation*, and it will be discussed in greater detail in Chapter 4.

One object can also be used as a basis for another object. For example, many car manufacturers use the same frame to make many different brands of cars by just changing their outside bodies. This is a concept called *inheritance* and will be discussed further in Chapter 5.

Why Objects Exist

An object is not based in procedure, meaning in other words, that if you create an object, you never know when that object will be used within a given program. With a procedural programming language such as COBOL, you know that the code will be executed in order; for example, that line one will be executed before the code on line two. With OOP you do not know when an object will be called or what part of the object will be used.

A good way of explaining these ideas is to consider a web page. Say, for instance, that you have a web page with two buttons and two text boxes. At the moment, it does not matter where the buttons or the text boxes are located, but it's important to understand that the two buttons and the two text boxes are objects for programming purposes. As a programmer, you don't know when or even if either of the buttons will be pushed, nor do you know if the text boxes will have text placed in them or not. This illustrates the fact that objects are not procedural in nature.

Within a given object, there *will* be actions that will be procedural in nature. For example, going back to the car object example, one action that can be taken on the car is to start the car. Within the action of starting the car, there are certain steps that must be done sequentially. So, within an object, there may be procedural-style programming, but the use of the object itself is not procedural. If you think about it, this very closely models the real world. Just because you get into your car doesn't mean that the car will automatically start, and just because you start the car doesn't mean the car will go forward immediately. In contrast to the real world, with OOP, all of these actions are independent of each other. Each individual action can be taken or called when necessary. You may want to just get into the car to get something out that you forgot, and in that case, the car should not start immediately and start moving forward. You may also be parked behind another car in a parking lot. You want to be able to start the car and put it in reverse instead of drive.

Objects As the Building Blocks of OOP

Objects are called the building blocks of OOP because a program written with an OOP language such as VB.NET may have many objects within it. Take, for example, a web site for scheduling college courses. There may be a student object with information about students, a room object with information about classrooms, a course object with information about courses, and finally a schedule object that holds information about the final schedule for each course in each room and the number of students in each course.

These objects are independent of one another but may be loosely tied together. For example, the schedule object would need to reference the other objects, since the schedule is made up of courses, rooms, and students. All of these objects could be written by the same programmer or split up to be written by a few different programmers. The programmer working on the schedule object would only need to know what information to give to and expect from the course object. She would not need to ask the course object programmer about the detailed code or how the object actually works. In fact, with the .NET Framework, it doesn't even matter which language each object was written in, because they will all work together as if written with the same language.

When programming the student object, the programmer doesn't know which particular actions pertaining to the student object that a future developer might take and in what order they might be used. For example, the student object might have two actions, one called CheckPrerequisites and another called CheckGradeLevel, which only come into play if the student is registering for classes. One or both of these actions might be taken to determine if the student qualifies for the course. However, it's also possible the course the student is attempting to enroll in doesn't have prerequisites, meaning that the schedule object wouldn't need to request that the course object perform the CheckPrerequisites action. Alternatively, it's possible that the school in question allows any student at any grade level to take a specific course. Therefore, the CheckGradeLevel action would not be required for that particular course, and the schedule object would not need to request that the course object perform the CheckGradeLevel action.

This has been yet another example showing that objects are not procedural. However, a programmer would still need to follow certain steps when writing the code for the CheckPrerequisites action. For example, the CheckPrerequisites action may require that the program first check to ensure the student is truly enrolled at the college, then determine if there is any money owed, and finally, make sure the student has passed the prerequisite course. If you can remember the last time you attempted to enroll in a course at a college, you will realize that these objects do model the real world. But keep in mind that for any given problem, the objects required and the actions required may be different.

The object (or in this case objects) really implements the business rules that are defined within the real world. For example, the CheckPrerequisites action mentioned in my college scheduling example performs checks that are defined by business rules. The business rules help to determine what actions to take and what steps are involved when performing actions.

Introduction to Reusability

Reusability is the concept of using the same object for multiple purposes and multiple applications. Reusability is really a by-product of OOP. The idea is that a single object should not be tied, or at most, very loosely tied, to other objects. This way the object can be used by any other object or client. (Loosely tied objects are objects that rely on one another but are not entirely dependent on one another.)

Importance of Reusability

Objects should be built to be reused as often as possible, because reusability helps to decrease development time. If an object that is known to work well and has been tested previously can be used in development, then valuable development time can be used for other purposes, rather than in creating new, redundant objects. As a rule of thumb, if there are multiple types of applications that are similar, there is a good chance that the code can be reused. Also, if you find yourself copying and pasting code from one application to another already, you can probably put that code into an object to be reused. Finally, an object can be used if an application requires certain services (such as printing services) that other applications can also use and that can be detailed in general terms. For example, a printing object could be created to send items to printers, but that particular printing object could also be used by many applications to send items to a printer, instead of each application including its own object code for printing.

It's a fact that in some applications, reusability may not be practical. For many applications there are multiple layers of objects. For example, you may have an object that is used to provide all services related to database manipulation. This object can be reused. However, if the same application has an object that is specific to itself, the object may not be able to be reused. Using the example of the course scheduling that I discussed in the last section, consider that the student object could be reused in other applications within the college if it contains actions other than those specific to scheduling. For example, the student object could be used to enroll students in the college or to keep track of financial aid for a specific student. However, the rooms object probably would not be useful in any other application within the college. These decisions are best made during the design of the application and must be looked at closely (I'll talk more about object design in Chapter 7).

Incorporating Reusability

Reusability can be very difficult to implement, especially within larger organizations. Within a small organization, there may be only one or two programmers, who are likely familiar with their own code and can easily recognize instances when another programmer might be able to use it to solve a specific problem. In larger organizations, reusability must be looked at from an enterprise level. Someone within the organization must break down the objects that are required for each application and then decide whether existing objects can be used or not. To make this easier, a set of reusable objects that perform the common actions specific to the organization should be kept in a library. This library can also be considered a *framework*.

A framework is a group of objects that are reusable and that may or may not depend on one another. Many companies (like mine) have a framework that includes all common objects that are used for applications. Objects that fit in this category are usually the "lower level" objects that provide for tasks that are common across most, if not all, of the applications within a company. The biggest problem with using a library or framework is that developers must have a central place to determine which objects exist within the library or framework and must have access to their documentation. Developers must also be able to determine whether there is an object that has already been built to perform the work that they need. Within the .NET Framework, this organization-specific library could be a *namespace* (collections of classes that are similar). I will discuss the concept of a namespace in Chapter 6.

The .NET Framework also provides an object library called the .NET Class Library. This is a library of many different objects that perform the common programming functions that most applications need. For example, there is the ActiveX Data Object (ADO) .NET object that is used for working with databases. This object provides services for connecting to a database as well as for getting information back out of databases. If this object did not exist, each application would need to have separate code in order to use the low level database provider to connect to the database. This would require more time for each application and would require a programmer with a greater knowledge of the low-level database provider. Instead, the ADO.NET object hides all of the ugly details from us. As you now know, this is called encapsulation, and you can find more about it in Chapter 4.

Introduction to OOP with .NET

The .NET Framework, and all of the programming languages for .NET, are based on the concepts of OOP. The .NET Framework itself is very reliant on the concepts of OOP. In this section I'll discuss which objects are within the .NET Framework and show you how to create objects within VB.NET.

Objects in .NET

Objects in .NET are called *classes*. Simply put, classes are another name for objects. The .NET Framework not only includes the Common Language Runtime (CLR), as mentioned earlier in the book, but also includes a class library. This class library contains a large number of predefined classes that are included to handle common programming tasks. These classes reflect the real world, just as any object does. For example, there is a class called SQLConnection that provides services for connecting to a database. This class simplifies the code that would need to be written each time an application needed to connect to a database. Therefore, this class is considered to be reusable. Most applications need to connect to a database and any application that connects to a SQL Server database will most likely use this class. The SQLConnection class is also a member of a larger organization of classes called a namespace. The System.Data.SQLClient namespace provides services for all database functionality. The System.Data.SQLClient.SQLConnection class is just one of those classes, and provides just a part of the overall functionality. Namespaces will be covered later in this chapter.

OBJECTS IN ASP.NET WEB APPLICATIONS

When creating ASP.NET web applications, everything is an object or class. The page that will hold user interface controls is a class, and the user controls themselves are classes. Again, each of the classes represents the real world. For example, consider the Page class, which is the container for all user interface elements. This class represents what users will see when interacting with the ASP.NET application. Any user interface element, such as a text box, is a class. All user interface elements have attributes and a core set of actions that they perform. Then, each specific type of user interface element adds actions and attributes that are specific to that type of element. For example, all of the elements have an ID attribute that corresponds to the name of the control. However, buttons have actions that determine what to do when a user clicks the button. The text box user interface element doesn't have an action that determines what to do when a user clicks the text box because it isn't necessary.

To illustrate this point, create a new file system web site (see Chapter 1 for instructions on doing this) that points to a folder on your computer called Chapter2, as shown in Figure 2-1.

Figure 2-1. *Creating a new file system web site called Chapter2*

Right-click on the Default.aspx file and choose View Code, as shown in Figure 2-2. This will open the code file Default.aspx.vb in the middle of the viewing area.

Click the down arrow for the drop-down on the top-left side of the page. It should say (General). From that list, choose (page_events). Now, click the down arrow for the drop-down list on the right. Choose Load from the right drop-down list. (The left drop-down is a list of classes, and for each class chosen from the left drop-down list there is a list of method or actions on the right.) Actions and attributes will be discussed in Chapter 3.

After you've completed the previous instructions, the first and last line of code for the action called Page_Load should have been created, as shown in Figure 2-3. Page_Load is an action that can be taken on the Page class. Basically any code you want to be executed when the page is loaded goes into this Sub.

Figure 2-2. *Choosing View Code to view the coding window*

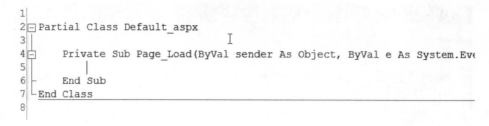

Figure 2-3. *The Page_Load action*

Using the Object Browser in Visual Studio 2005

The Object Browser is a tool within Visual Studio that shows you all of the objects that are part of a project or application. This includes all of the objects that are part of the .NET Class Library within the .NET Framework. Using the Object Browser will give you a chance to see all of the objects that you can use and also give you some insight into how objects can model the real world.

To access the Object Browser, choose View ➤ Object Browser, as shown in Figure 2-4. The Object Browser will appear in the middle of the screen.

The first screen of the Object Browser will display all of the namespaces within the .NET Class Library. A namespace is essentially a collection of classes (and remember that classes are objects). Namespaces will be covered in more depth in Chapter 6.

Double-click on the System.Windows.Forms namespace within the Object Browser, as shown in Figure 2-5. This will expand the current namespace and show other namespaces located within that namespace.

Find the System.Windows.Forms namespace and double-click it. You will see a long list of items, as shown in Figure 2-6.

The items with the multicolored icons (such as AccessibleObject in Figure 2-6) are classes. If you go down the list and click on some of the various classes, you'll see the area to the right of the class list fill up with a list of actions and attributes. Click the class called Button under the System. Windows.Forms namespace and the list of actions and attributes for the Button class will appear on the right, as in Figure 2-7.

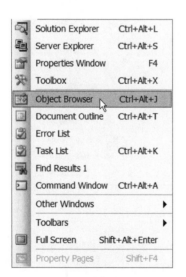

Figure 2-4. *Choosing Object Browser from the View menu*

Figure 2-7. *The actions and attributes of the Button class*

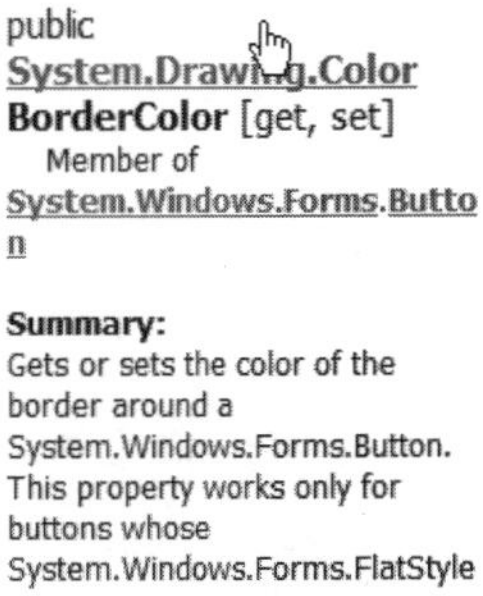

Figure 2-5. *Choosing System.Windows.Forms from the Object Browser*

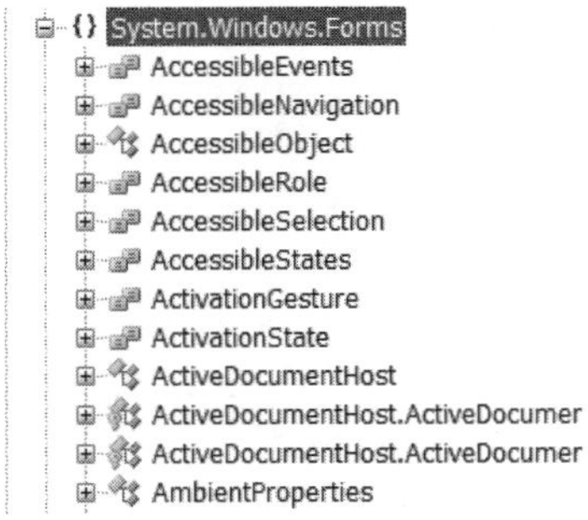

Figure 2-6. *Part of the System.Windows.Forms namespace*

public **System.Drawing.Color BorderColor** [get, set]
     Member of
System.Windows.Forms.Button

Summary:
Gets or sets the color of the border around a System.Windows.Forms.Button. This property works only for buttons whose System.Windows.Forms.FlatStyle

Figure 2-8. *More information about the BorderColor attribute*

The items that have a purple icon next to them are actions, while the items with a hand beside them are "public" attributes. The items with the blue icons beside them are the "private" attributes of the classes. If you click on one of these attributes or actions, some more information about the item will appear in the small box below the attribute and action list. For example, click on the BorderColor attribute with the hand icon beside it (meaning the public Border-Color attribute). You'll see that more information for that attribute will appear below the list, as shown in Figure 2-8.

If you continue to scroll up and down, clicking on classes and namespaces, you will see that there are hundreds of classes and thousands of attributes and actions. These are all part of the .NET Framework. It's not necessary to memorize any of these. Many of these items are used behind the scenes by the .NET Framework. For example, when you create a new web application, the default page created is automatically based on the Page class.

Creating a Class with VB.NET

This is the moment you have been waiting for. You may have been asking yourself, "What does all of this mean to me? I just want to create a web site!"

Up to this point, I have covered the theory behind the objects that are the classes within VB.NET, and I've covered the objects that exist within the .NET Class Library. Now that you have some background information, it's time to create a web site with VB.NET. The first step is to create your very first class. To create a new class within VB.NET, right-click the name of the project at the top of the Solution Explorer (should be c:\chapter2) and choose Add New Item. From the Add New Item window, choose Class, as shown in Figure 2-9, and then enter **MyFirstClass** in the name field. Next, click Add.

■**Note** If you do not see the Solution Explorer, it may be closed or hidden. If the Solution Explorer is closed, click the View menu, then choose Solution Explorer to view the Solution Explorer again. The Solution Explorer is hidden at the right edge of the screen. Move your mouse over to the tab for the Solution Explorer to expand it.

Figure 2-9. *Choosing Class from the Add New Items window*

After you click Add for the new class, a window will appear (shown in Figure 2-10), asking if you want to create a code directory. Click Yes.

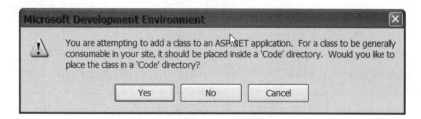

Figure 2-10. *Adding a Code directory*

Your new class will be created and the code window will now appear in the middle of the screen. The actual file name will be MyFirstClass.vb and it will be visible in the Solution Explorer on the right. Do not remove the two lines of code that are added by default. Every class must begin with a declaration line that includes the name and access modifier (Public in this case) and every class must end with an End Class.

Enter the following code between the existing lines:

```
Public Function ReturnString() As String
        Return "Myclass"
End Function
```

This code will create a function (or action) that will return a string value of general text to the code that requests this action. The first line of this code is the *action declaration*, which defines what action to take. The first line of this code is the only information that other code wanting to perform the ReturnString action of the MyFirstClass object will see.

Using a Class in VB.NET

After adding an action to the class, you can now *use* the class. To use a class, a variable must first be created with a data type that matches the class name. Click on the Default.aspx.vb tab to add code to the page. The Page_Load action of the page should still be visible. If not, click the left drop-down list at the top of the window, choose Page Events, and then choose Load from the drop-down list on the right. Add the following lines of code on the line after the Page_Load declaration line:

```
Private Sub Form1_Load(ByVal sender As System.Object, ByVal e As
System.EventArgs)➡
Handles Form1.Load
        Dim clsMy As New MyFirstClass
        Dim strReturn As String
End Sub
```

The first line of code (carrying on to the second line in the previous example) is the sub declaration. The second line of code (starting with dim clsMy as New MyFirstClass) declares a variable called clsMy that is an instance of the MyFirstClass class, and this declaration will make an exact copy of MyFirstClass. The third line will declare a variable that is a string, to hold a string value.

Now add this line of code below the other two:

```
strreturn = clsMy.ReturnString
```

This line of code will accept the value from the ReturnString action and will then ask the MyFirstClass class to perform the action and provide a string value back. I'll discuss how actions and attributes are defined and used in Chapter 3.

Now that all of the code has been added, place a breakpoint on the line that requests the instance of MyFirstClass to perform the ReturnString action (strreturn=clsMy.ReturnString). This will allow you to walk through the code as the application executes. You can do this by clicking the gray area to the left of the line so that a maroon bar appears over the line. You can start to debug the application by choosing Start from the Debug menu. If you do this, you may be told that a configuration file must be created first. Click OK and the page should begin to load in a Web browser. Next, the code page should appear with a yellow line over the breakpoint, as shown in Figure 2-11.

```
 1
 2  Partial Class Default_aspx
 3
 4      Private Sub Page_Load(ByVal sender As Object, ByVal e As System.E
 5          Dim clsMy As New MyFirstClass
 6          Dim strreturn As String
 7
 8          strreturn = clsMy.ReturnString
 9      End Sub
10  End Class
11
```

Figure 2-11. *Breakpoint on the action callck*

When the breakpoint appears, press the F11 key. This will actually transfer the debugger to within the MyFirstClass file, since the F11 key tells the debugger to move to the next line of code, as shown in Figure 2-12.

```
 1  Imports Microsoft.VisualBasic
 2
 3  Public Class MyFirstClass
 4      Public Function ReturnString() As String
 5          ReturnString = "Myclass"
 6      End Function
 7  End Class
 8
```

Figure 2-12. *Debugger transferring to MyFirstClass file*

Press F11 again and the debugger will be on the line `ReturnString="MyClass"`. This line will assign the string "MyClass" to the action that was performed, which in turn will send that value ("MyClass") back to the variable called strreturn within the Page_Load action. Press F11 two more times to leave both this action and MyFirstClass.

Now the debugger will be back within the Page_Load action again. Press the F11 key one more time to complete the assignment. Place your mouse over strreturn and you should see that the value "MyClass" has been assigned to that variable.

A very important point about the use of classes is that each instance of a class is unique. That is, if you had declared two variables, clsMy and clsMy1, both as an instance of the MyFirstClass, both would hold an independent copy of MyFirstClass. But remember that the values assigned to one instance may not be the same as the ones assigned to the second. For example, if you had a class with an attribute that could provide a random value, and you created two instances of this class, you would find that both have a different random value.

Conclusion

In this chapter I introduced objects, the core concept of OOP. I showed you why objects are necessary, and discussed the importance of reusability in development. I also gave you an introduction to classes within VB.NET.

CHAPTER 3

■■■

Attributes and Actions

I'll begin this chapter by taking a look at what attributes and actions are within OOP and then show you how to create attributes and actions using VB.NET.

Attributes

Attributes, in OOP, are a way to describe the characteristics of a real-world entity. In my car example from Chapter 2, the color of the car is an attribute. You can allow attributes to change, or not, depending on how you use them. When a real-world entity needs to be translated into an object, the attributes usually follow the descriptive words of the real-world entity. For example, a business process may state that the car must be red in color, must have four wheels, and must have mobility. The car, in this case, is the noun, so it's the object. The first adjective (descriptive word) I've used is "red." The attribute is the thing that follows the descriptive word, which in the case of the car is color.

In many business processes the descriptive words may not be actually followed by an attribute. Instead, you may need to infer the attribute, which makes the job of defining attributes more difficult. In the previous example, the business process might state that the car must be red, have four wheels, and be able to both go and not go, as needed. This business process appears to be very good, because the process is giving you the specifics of an object. However, the business process mentioned is specific to one instance of an object (called a *class* in VB.NET). Given this example, you must determine what the attribute is. Are the attributes red and four? This is a case where you need to infer the attributes. Based on your knowledge of the real world, you could probably determine that among the attributes for a car are color and wheels. However, if you aren't as familiar with the business process, you may need to ask more questions, such as, in this case, what "red" is in terms of the car. I'll discuss how to design classes based on business process information in Chapter 7.

Actions

Actions, in OOP, are a way to define what a real-world entity does. Using the car example from Chapter 2, let's consider the idea that the car moves forward and backwards. Actions are typically verbs within a business process. If the business process dictates that the car must be red in color, have four wheels, and start and stop, note that start and stop are verbs, and therefore actions. Based on your knowledge of the real world, you would already know that a car can start and stop. In this way, actions are a little easier to determine than attributes when designing a class, because they are typically the verbs in a business process.

As you will see in Chapter 7, there may be other actions required of an object besides the obvious ones that you get from the business process. There also may be underlying actions that need to be performed before the actions specified in the business process can be performed. With the car example, the action of the driver pressing down the brake pedal may need to be performed before the stop action can take place. That isn't obvious from the original business process, but you know that in the real world, if the driver does not press the brake, the car will neither stop nor attempt to stop (meaning that the stop action is not taken). Finding these hidden actions can be very difficult and can sometimes only be defined during the design or development phase of a project.

Attributes and Actions Within VB.NET

In this section, I'll cover how attributes and actions defined within OOP are implemented in VB.NET.

VB.NET Properties

Within VB.NET, attributes of an object are called *properties*. Just like attributes, properties describe the object. Properties are found the same way that attributes are found within the business process.

Properties within a class have a data type associated with them, just as variables do. This data type must be given to the property when it is first defined within a class. The data type can be any valid data type within the VB.NET language.

■Note The data type you choose for a property may restrict the type of information that can be assigned to that property. For example, if you have data that can be either whole numbers or decimal numbers, you need to define that property as decimal. If you previously defined that property as an integer (whole number), but then attempted to assign a decimal value to it, only the whole number part of the value would be stored. To help prevent this, set Option Strict on as mentioned in the next section.

Properties within a class have an access modifier. Access modifiers are ways to restrict the use of a property or variable. The four main access modifiers for properties are public, private, readonly, and writeonly. Public properties are available to *any* code using an instance of the class, while private properties are available only to the class. Readonly properties can only be read from the class and writeonly properties can only be written to the class.

Adding Properties to a VB.NET Class

Properties are most commonly defined with a variable and a property. I know I've said previously that properties and variables are the same thing, but in this case it's *how* you define the access modifier that determines the difference. A very common way to create properties is to have a private variable defined within the class. Again, a private variable defined within a specific class can only be used within that class. Any code attempting to use the class will not be able to directly manipulate this private variable. The manipulation of this private variable is allowed via the creation of a public property. Any code wanting to use the class will use the public property to access the value in the private variable.

A class may be defined in the following manner, with both a public property and private variable:

```
Public Class Car
Private strColor as String
    Public Property Color() As String
        Get
            Return strColor
        End Get
        Set(ByVal value As String)
            strColor = value
        End Set
    End Property
End Class
```

In this example, the variable strColor is private to the class and therefore cannot be accessed from outside the class. If you have created an instance of this class (as we will do in the following sections), the strColor variable would not be available to you because it has been marked as private. The Color public property would be available for your use, however, since it's marked as public. The public property Color is also defined as a data type string, which means that it will accept alphanumeric information. The Get group of statements returns a value when an instance of the class attempts to access the Color public property. When an instance of this class attempts to assign a value to the Color public property, the Set group of statements will assign the value given to the private strColor variable.

Using the private variable and public property setup, as I've just defined, gives you the advantage of adding more code to the Get and Set statements that validates the incoming or outgoing data or does other things with the data that you might not be able to do otherwise.

Another way to present the properties of a class is to just define all variables as public:

```
Public Class Car
    Public strColor as string
End Class
```

Defined in this way, an instance of the class *would* be able to access the strColor variable, because that variable is now public. Any code using an instance of the class in this situation would have direct access to the variable that the class code will use to perform its tasks. Many developers use this kind of coding to save time, because defining private variables and public properties individually takes more time. I prefer not to assign all values via public variables, but rather define my variables with a standard naming convention. For example, all string variables begin with str. If I define all of my variables that way, and define them as public instead of private, then reusability becomes more difficult. Defining private variables and public properties makes reusability easier because by defining the public property as private, you can also give the property a more recognizable name. In my previous examples, you saw that the public property was called Color and the private variable was strColor. In this example, both the private variable and the public property would have the same meaning to someone writing code against your class. However, you may want to define the private variable with one name and the public property with a different one. Here I show the private variable with one name and the public property with a friendlier name:

```
Public Class Car
    Private blnCarStarted as boolean
    Public Property CarIsStarted as boolean
        Get
            Return blnCarStarted
        End Get
        Set(ByVal value As String)
            blnCarStarted = value
        End Set
    End Property
End Class
```

Here you can see that the private variable blnCarStarted might have the same name as the column in the database holding the value. To make the class easier to use for others, you may want to change the public property to a more easily understood name, such as CarIsStarted. When another developer using your class wants to let the class know whether the car is started or not, the developer will assign either true or false to the CarIsStarted public property.

This code is also an example of the encapsulation concept, which was introduced in Chapter 2 and will be further explained in Chapter 4. By making your variables private, you can hide (encapsulate) how the class's actual work is done.

Using a Class Public Property in VB.NET

Now that you understand how to add a public property to a class, you need to know how to use the public property. I am now going to move away from the car example and try to present something more relevant to business. So, for the subsequent sections in this chapter, I will be working with a common business process: allowing an employee to enter his or her first name, last name, and date of birth. This could be for any type of application, such as a help desk ticket, a benefits form, or even payroll information.

In this business process, the employee is the noun, and therefore the object, and will become the class name. The attributes in this example are the employee's first name, last name, and date of birth. These attributes will become the properties of the class.

First, create a new web site called Chapter3 (see Chapter 1 for more information on how to create a new web site). Leave the Default.aspx page as it is and add a new class, called Employee, to the web site (see Chapter 2 for details on how to do this).

Within the `Public Class Employee` and `End Class` lines, define two string variables: strFirstName and strLastName. Then, add a private date variable called dteDateOfBirth. The resulting code would look like

```
Public Class Employee
    Private strFirstName as String
    Private strLastName as String
    Private dteDateOfBirth as Date
End Class
```

These are the private variables that will be used by the Employee class, but will not be accessible to new code using the class. Next, create the public properties within the Employee class for FirstName, LastName, and DateOfBirth. A quick way to do this is to type **Public Property** and then the public property name, followed by "As" and the type of variable (i.e., `Public Property FirstName as String`) and hit Enter. VS2005 will create the required structures for you:

```
Public Class Employee
    Private strFirstName As String
    Private strLastName As String
    Private dteDateOfBirth As Date
```

```
    Public Property FirstName() As String
        Get
            Return strFirstName
        End Get
        Set(ByVal value As String)
            strFirstName = value
        End Set
    End Property
    Public Property LastName() As String
        Get
            Return strLastName
        End Get
        Set(ByVal value As String)
            strLastName = value
        End Set
    End Property
    Public Property DateOfBirth() As Date
        Get
            Return dteDateOfBirth
        End Get
        Set(ByVal value As Date)
            dteDateOfBirth = value
        End Set
    End Property
End Class
```

Note the As Date part of the declaration of the DateOfBirth public property. This is an example of the restriction of data types that you can implement with public properties. If a value is passed to the public property that is not of type Date, the call will fail. To help prevent this error from occurring, set Option Strict On by choosing Options from the Tools Menu within Visual Studio. Once there, open the Projects and Solutions folder and choose VB Defaults. Change the Option Strict setting to On.

Now open Default.aspx.vb, the code file for the Default.aspx page. Choose Page Events from the drop-down list on the top left of the Code Designer and then choose Load from the drop-down on the top right. Your code page should look like this:

```
Partial Class Default_aspx

Private Sub Page_Load(ByVal sender As Object, ByVal e As System.EventArgs)
Handles Me.Load

End Sub
End Class
```

Now, declare a local variable called clsEmployee of type Employee within the Page_Load sub:

```
Partial Class Default_aspx

Private Sub Page_Load(ByVal sender As Object, ByVal e As System.EventArgs)
Handles Me.Load
Dim clsEmployee as New Employee
End Sub
End Class
```

This declaration (Dim clsEmployee as New Employee) will create a new instance of the Employee class. On the next line, you can either type **ClsEmployee** or **clsE**, while holding down the Ctrl key and hitting the space bar. When you hold down the Ctrl key and hit the space bar, VS2005 automatically completes the variable name for you. Notice that IntelliSense only shows the public properties, though—it doesn't show strFirstName, strLastName, or dteDateofBirth. This is because you have defined those variables as private, so they can't be accessed by other code using the class. After choosing ClsEmployee, choose FirstName, and then add an equals sign. Next, add your first name in quotes. On the next line, go through the same process with your last name and date of birth (I'll use a fake date of birth):

```
Partial Class Default_aspx

Private Sub Page_Load(ByVal sender As Object, ByVal e As System.EventArgs)
Handles Me.Load
    Dim clsEmployee as New Employee
    clsEmployee.FirstName = "Brian"
    clsEmployee.LastName = "Myers"
    clsEmployee.DateOfBirth = "1/1/1900"
End Sub
End Class
```

NOTE After entering the date of birth, you may see a gray squiggle line under the value 1/1/1900. If you mouse over this you will see that this is an implicit conversion between string and date. The squiggle line just lets you know that VB.NET will be converting the string value (between quotes) to a date value.

These lines of code will assign a value to each of the public properties of the class. To better see how this works, place a breakpoint on the first line of the assignment code (clsEmployee.FirstName = "Brian"). Next, click the Debug menu and choose Start. This will begin debugging the application (click OK when asked to add a web.config file). When the breakpoint is activated, as shown in Figure 3-1, press the F11 key.

```
 1
 2 ⊟ Partial Class Default_aspx                                          I
 3
 4 ⊟     Private Sub Page_Load(ByVal sender As Object, ByVal e As System.E
 5           Dim clsEmployee As New Employee
 6           clsEmployee.FirstName = "Brian"
 7           clsEmployee.LastName = "Myers"
 8           clsEmployee.DateOfBirth = "1/1/1900"
 9
10  ⌐    End Sub
11  └ End Class
12
```

Figure 3-1. *Activated breakpoint*

After you press F11, the application execution will go to the Set statement of the Employee Class Public Property FirstName, as shown in Figure 3-2.

```
 7
 8 ⊟     Public Property FirstName() As String
 9 ⊟         Get
10              Return StrFirstName
11  ⌐         End Get
12 ⊟         Set(ByVal value As String)
13              StrFirstName = value
14  ⌐         End Set
15  ⌐     End Property
16 ⊟     Public Property LastName() As String
17 ⊟         Get
18              Return StrLastName
19  ⌐         End Get
20 ⊟         Set(ByVal value As String)
21              StrLastName = value
22  ⌐         End Set
23  ⌐     End Property
```

Figure 3-2. *Set statement of the FirstName public property*

Press F11 to move to the assignment statement, and then press F11 again to move to the End Set statement. If you mouse over the strFirstName variable in the line strFirstName = value, you will see that the value of strFirstName is now the name that you assigned to it (in my case, this is "Brian"). Pressing F11 yet again will take you back to the Page_Load sub of the Default.aspx page. You can stop debugging by clicking the Debug menu and then selecting Stop Debugging.

VB.NET Methods

Actions within OOP are implemented as either functions or subs within VB.NET. Subs and functions are smaller groupings of code that perform a specific task. Subs do not return a value, while functions do. A public function or sub is called a Method. For instance, with our car example, one method might be start and another stop.

Functions and subs within a class have the same class-specific access modifiers that properties and local variables do. A *public* function or sub is considered a method because it is exposed to other code using the class. A *private* function or sub is still considered a function or sub, rather than a method, since the private function or sub is not exposed to any code outside of the class.

Every class has a *constructor,* which is a sub that is called when an instance of the class is created. You can add code to this sub if you want a task to be performed each time an instance of the class is created. For example, you might want to add code to the constructor that allows the initialization of some values when the class is created. Using our car example from before, the constructor would be the same as getting in the car. That must be accomplished before any of the other car actions (such as start) can take place.

Parameters in VB.NET

Functions and subs within VB.NET were introduced in the last section, but in this section I'll expand on what you learned and show you the usage of ByVal and ByRef.

A sample function and sub follow:

```
Public Function ValueSwitch() as Boolean
Public Sub ValueSwitch()
```

There are two ways to get data into a function or sub. First, you can define public properties within the class that will accept values *before* the function or sub is called. The problem with this approach is if the function or sub is dependent on the value, and the public properties are not set before the function or sub is called, the function or sub will fail. This approach will work, however, if your class is specific to an application and if you are the only one working on that application.

The other approach is to use parameters, sending a value when calling the function or sub, to pass important values into the function or sub. If a parameter is defined, the function or sub can't be called unless a value is provided for said parameter. Therefore, there is no chance that the function or sub will be called without a value provided. The value may not be correct, or even in a correct range, but it must be both provided and provided in the correct data type in order for the function or sub to be called. Here is a sub and function that contains a parameter:

```
Public Function ValueSwitch(ByVal FirstValue as integer) as Boolean
Public Sub ValueSwitch(ByVal FirstValue as integer)
```

Parameters can be passed either ByRef (by reference) or ByVal (by value). The default, and the option used by programmers most of the time, is ByVal.

ByVal is the code equivalent to a one-way street. Though the value given to the parameter is passed into the function or sub to be used, the function or sub doesn't change the parameter value. Instead, the function or sub receives a copy of the value in the variable and therefore cannot change the actual value.

ByRef is the equivalent of a two-way street. The value you give to the parameter may be changed by the function or sub and used again when calling the code. The parameter itself is really a pointer to the actual value of the parameter, unlike ByVal, which just gives a copy of the value. Using parameters within functions and subs will be covered more in the next section.

Adding Methods in VB.NET

Methods within VB.NET are implemented as either functions or subs. A public function or sub is considered a method because it is exposed to the code that is using the class. To create a method, simply create a function or sub as public.

In our car example from previous sections, a function could be created for the Start action. The class code begins with the declaration of a private variable and a public property:

```
Public Class Car
    Private strColor as String
    Public Property color() As String
        Get
            Return strcolor
        End Get
        Set(ByVal value As String)
            strcolor = value
        End Set
    End Property
End Class
```

Next, a function is added after the public property called Start, which returns a Boolean value to determine if the car has really started or not:

```
Public Class Car
    Private strColor as String
    Public Property Color() As String
        Get
            Return strcolor
        End Get
```

```
      Set(ByVal value As String)
          strcolor = value
      End Set
   End Property
Public Function Start () as Boolean

End Function
End Class
```

NOTE Each function or sub declaration must be concluded with an End Function. When you are typing this into Visual Studio (as I will do in the next section), if you hit the Enter key after typing the function or sub declaration, the End Function or End Sub will automatically be created.

The code you need to make the car start should go between the declaration statement, Public Function Start() as Boolean, and the End Function statement. Since this is a function, it must return a value; for that, use the Return statement. In this case, the value must be either True or False, and the function would look like this:

```
Public Function Start () as Boolean
              Return True
End Function
```

To create a function or sub that accepts parameters, define the name of the parameter and the data type within the parentheses following the name of the function or sub:

```
Public Function Start (ByVal NumberofTries as Integer) as Boolean
              Return True
End Function
Public Sub Start (ByVal NumberofTries as Integer)

End Sub
```

Using a Method in VB.NET

This section will expand the employee class that you created in the "Using a Class Public Property in VB.NET" section. In this business process, there is also a requirement that the employee's first and last name be *concatenated* together (or added together as one string of characters).

To begin, open the web site called Chapter3 if you haven't already opened it. If you didn't create this web site previously, you'll need to do so now. Once you open the web site, click on and open the Employee class file called Employee.vb. At the end of the class, just before the End Class statement, add a function called ConCatNames. This function should accept two parameters, both the first name and last name, and then return the concatenated name:

```
Public Function ConCatNames(FirstName as string,LastName as string) as string
        Return Firstname & LastName
End Function
End Class
```

Now, open the code page for the Default page (Default.aspx.vb). Declare a new variable called strConCatName as a string. Declare a new variable called strFirstName as a string, and then declare another new variable called strLastName as a string. Add a statement assigning a value to strFirstName and strLastName after the assignment statements that are already there, then add the following call to the ConCatNames function:

```
strConCatName = clsEmployee.ConCatNames(strFirstName,strLastName)
```

Your code under the Page_Load section should look like Figure 3-3.

```
 1
 2 tial Class Default_aspx
 3
 4   Private Sub Page_Load(ByVal sender As Object, ByVal e As System.Event
 5        Dim clsEmployee As New Employee
 6        Dim StrConCatName As String
 7        Dim StrFirstName As String
 8        Dim StrLastName As String
 9
10        clsEmployee.FirstName = "Brian"
11        clsEmployee.LastName = "Myers"
12        clsEmployee.DateOfBirth = "1/1/1900"
13
14        StrFirstName = "Brian"
15        StrLastName = "Myers"
16        StrConCatName = clsEmployee.ConCatName(StrFirstName, StrLastName)
17
18   End Sub
19   Class
20
```

Figure 3-3. *Completed code for Page_Load*

Next, place a breakpoint on line 14 (strFirstName="Brian") and then debug the application (Debug Menu ➤ Start). When the execution of the application comes to the breakpoint, hit the F11 key to move to the next line. Next, hit the F11 key to move the call to the ConCatName function at line 16. Press the F11 key again to move into the ConCatName function within the Employee class. Then, press the F11 key again to move to the assignment statement, and then again to move to the End Function line. Press F11 again to return to the code in the Default.aspx page. Finally, press F11 one last time to move off the call and to the End Sub line (line 18).

Now place your mouse over the variable strConCatName and you will see that the value is now the concatenation of the strFirstName and strLastName values (in my case, BrianMyers). You can stop the debugging by clicking the Debug menu and then choosing Stop Debugging.

You should glean a few important things from this example. First, you will notice that when you are calling the function on the Default.aspx page, the parameters are strFirstName and strLastName. Within the Employee class, however, the parameters are FirstName and LastName:

```
strConCatName = clsEmployee.ConCatNames(ByVal strFirstName,By Val strLastName)
Public Function ConCatNames➡
(ByVal FirstName as string,ByVal LastName as string) as string
```

The names of the parameters and variables that are passing the values to the parameters aren't important to this process. What is important is that both the function declaration (within the class) and the call to the function (the code using the class) use the same data types for the parameters. As long as you make sure that the string value is defined with the function there is little that can cause a problem. But, for example, if the function has a parameter with a data type of Date and you attempt to pass an integer value to the function, an error will occur.

Now I am going to change the ConCatNames function to a sub by changing its type from Function to Sub and removing the return value declaration (as string):

```
Public Sub ConCatNames(ByVal FirstName as string,ByVal LastName as string)
```

Within the ConCatNames sub, remove the assignment line (ConCatNames = strFirstName & strLastName). Add a new parameter, ByRef, to the end of the parameter list called FullName. The sub declaration within the employee class would look like the following statement:

```
Public Sub ConCatNames➡
(ByVal FirstName as string,ByValLastName as string,ByRef FullName)
```

Add a new assignment line that concatenates the FirstName and LastName parameters and assigns that value to the FullName parameter:

```
FullName = FirstName & LastName
```

Since FullName is a parameter with a ByRef option, the value passed into the parameter can be modified by the function and the value doesn't need to be returned through a function (remember the two-way street idea). The completed function definition for ConCatNames would be as follows:

```
Public Sub ConCatName(ByVal FirstName As String, ByVal LastName As➨
String, ByRef FullName As String)
    FullName = FirstName & LastName
End Sub
```

Now go back to the code page for Default.aspx, called Default.aspx.vb. You'll notice that there is now a squiggle line under the call to ConCatName. First, add a new assignment line under strLastName, which should read strConCatName = "", completely remove the line that calls ConCatName, and then replace it with the new call:

```
clsEmployee.ConCatName(strFirstName, strLastName, strConCatName)
```

The completed code will look like Figure 3-4.

```
 1
 2 ⊟ ial Class Default_aspx
 3
 4 ⊟ Private Sub Page_Load(ByVal sender As Object, ByVal e As System.EventA⟩
 5       Dim clsEmployee As New Employee
 6       Dim StrConCatName As String
 7       Dim StrFirstName As String
 8       Dim StrLastName As String
 9
10       clsEmployee.FirstName = "Brian"
11       clsEmployee.LastName = "Myers"
12       clsEmployee.DateOfBirth = "1/1/1900"
13
14       StrFirstName = "Brian"
15       StrLastName = "Myers"
16       StrConCatName = ""
17       clsEmployee.ConCatName(StrFirstName, StrLastName, StrConCatName)
18
19  ⊦End Sub
20  ⌐Class
```

Figure 3-4. *Revised code for Page_Load*

Next, place a breakpoint on line 14 (strFirstName = "Brian") and debug the application by choosing Debug Menu ➤ Start. When the execution stops at the breakpoint, hit the F11 key to move to the strLastName assignment line and then F11 again to move to the strConCatName assignment line. Hit the F11 key to move to the call to ConCatName and then move your mouse over the strConCatName variable in the parameter list. Note that there is no value (value = Nothing). Now, hit the F11 key again to move into the sub and then again to move into the assignment statement. Next, hit the F11 key to move to the End Sub statement. Now, place your mouse over the FullName parameter in the parameter list and notice there is now a value (in my case BrianMyers). Hit the F11 key one more time to move back to the Default.aspx.vb file, and then again to move to the

End Sub on the Page_Load. Move your mouse over the strConCatName parameter in the parameters list and notice that it now also has a value, and that the value is the same as the FullName parameter was when the execution was inside the ConCatName sub.

Overloading

Overloading basically allows multiple functions or subs to exist with the same name but different parameters. This is most useful when you are unsure of the parameters that will be provided and there are values that are not required. An example of the code used to define a set of overloaded functions would look like this:

```
Public Function OverLoaded () as Boolean
Public Function OverLoaded (By Val Parameter1 as string) as Boolean
```

You can have more than two functions with the same name when you are overloading. Actually, there can be as many as you want, as long as they all have the same name, the same access modifier (public, private, and so on), and the same return value. Using our car example again, the car might have two methods for moving forward. The first method might not have any parameters and would be the same as moving forward in an automatic car. The second method might have a parameter for gear that would make it the same as moving forward in a standard car (with a gear shift). The gear parameter itself would then have a value of which gear to put the vehicle into, such as first, second, or third.

Conclusion

In this chapter I covered the implementation of attributes as properties in classes and the implementation of actions as methods. I also covered the creation of properties and methods within VB.NET. In the next chapter, I'll go over the concept of encapsulation and how it is implemented in VB.NET.

■■■

CHAPTER 4

Encapsulation

In this chapter, I'll cover the concept of encapsulation and show how it is implemented within VB.NET.

A General Overview of Encapsulation and Information Hiding

Encapsulation is a way to group methods (actions) and properties (data) into one unit and then control how these properties are changed and these methods are used. *Information hiding* is the idea that an object should not expose its data directly, but instead provide another mechanism to allow clients indirect access to the data.

Encapsulation and information hiding provide two advantages. First, other objects (sometimes known as client objects) can use an encapsulated object without knowing the inner workings of the encapsulated object. Even if the inner workings of a properly encapsulated object change, the encapsulated object will still function as it did before. This means that the client object will continue to function with the encapsulated object the same way as well. If the object is not properly encapsulated, the client objects would break when the object was changed.

The second advantage is that the implementation of the encapsulated object is not accessible by the client object. In this scenario, all the private variables and subroutines aren't known to a client object because of information hiding. If you like, you can think of an encapsulated object as a black box. You provide information to it, in the form of necessary parameters, and you receive the return value if there is one. In the meantime, you don't know what the encapsulated object is doing to perform the work, but you know that the work will be completed. The main reason for using information hiding is for situations where you know that if the method was readily available it might be broken by another developer who was attempting to tweak it. Information hiding is really a double-edged sword. If you need to perform an action similar to an action already taken by an object, but you want a different value returned or you want to provide a different parameter for it, with information hiding implemented on your object you couldn't do that. More importantly, you wouldn't be able to determine how the work was done, so you couldn't determine how to retrofit the method to accept your parameter or return a different value to you in the first place.

Since encapsulation makes the methods and properties of an object work as a unit, you can create two instances of the same object, provide different values to a given property of each instance, and then use that property without the two instances crossing. Consider this case: object A and object B are both instances of the object called Math. You assign a value of 4 to a property called InValue for object A, and you assign a value of 8 to the property called InValue for object B. The Math object has a method called MultiplyBySelf that multiplies the InValue property and returns the result as an integer. When you execute the MultiplyBySelf method of object A, the result would be 16. However, when you execute the MultiplyBySelf method of object B, the result would be 64. Thus the two objects are completely separate from each other.

Encapsulation in VB.NET

Say you are a developer within a large company. Many of the applications built by the company will require more complex mathematical equations. You need to create a class called Math that implements the functionality I mentioned previously. Of course there is nothing complex about this functionality, but it's a good way to show you the ideas behind encapsulation and information hiding. This class could be a part of a much larger company class library. However, to make the example simpler the class will be a single class that is built into an assembly (.dll file) to be used by other applications.

Keep in mind, you do not need to create a separate project for each class you want to create. You could create the class within the same project; however, in this case you want to create the class for all applications within your company to use. The best way to do that is to create a single assembly that can be referenced by other projects (referencing will be covered later in this chapter). You can also follow these steps if you want to create a class library for your company to facilitate reuse within your organization.

Getting Started

To begin, you need to create a class file and build it into an assembly (.dll file) to be used by a web application. To do this, open VS2005 and choose File ➤ New ➤ Project. The New Project window will then appear. Select Visual Basic as the language from the left-hand side. Then choose Class Library from the right. Change the project name to Encapsulation and place this class in a folder called C:\Encapsulation, as shown in Figure 4-1. Click OK when all the information has been added.

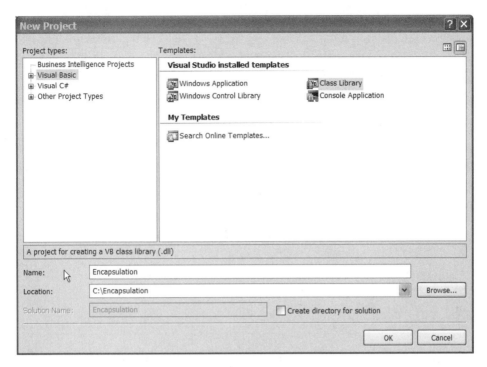

Figure 4-1. *Creating a new class library called Encapsulation*

Your class library is now called Encapsulation. Open the Solution Explorer, right-click on the Class1.vb file, and choose Rename as shown in Figure 4-2.

Figure 4-2. *Renaming Class1.vb*

Rename the Class1.vb file to Math.vb and notice that the class name changed on the left side as well (within the code area). Now add a private integer variable called intValue and then create a public property called InValue that is also an integer. To do this, in the code window under the class declaration (Public Class Math), add `Private intValue as Integer`. On the next line type `Public Property InValue as Integer` and hit the Enter key. VS2005 will automatically create the Set and Get methods for you. The resulting code should look like Figure 4-3.

```
1  Public Class Math
2      Private intValue As Integer
3      Public Property InValue() As Integer
4          Get
5
6          End Get
7          Set(ByVal value As Integer)
8
9          End Set
0      End Property
```

Figure 4-3. *Public and Private property*

Now between Get and End Get, enter `Return intValue`. Between the Set and End Set lines, type `intValue = value`. The resulting code should look like Figure 4-4.

```
Public Class Math
    Private intValue As Integer
    Public Property InValue() As Integer
        Get
            Return intValue
        End Get
        Set(ByVal value As Integer)
            intValue = value
        End Set
    End Property
```

Figure 4-4. *Completed Public Property code*

Figure 4-5 shows the concept of information hiding. There is a private variable called intValue that the class Math will use. There is a public property called InValue that other classes wanting to interact with the Math class will use to either provide a value or retrieve the current value. An advantage to creating public properties this way not yet mentioned is that you can write validation code in the Get and Set methods if necessary. Figure 4-5 shows the use of validation in the Set method.

```
Public Class Math
    Private intValue As Integer
    Public Property InValue() As Integer
        Get
            Return intValue
        End Get
        Set(ByVal value As Integer)
            If intValue > 0 Then
                intValue = value
            Else
                Throw New Exception("InValue can not be less than 1")
            End If
        End Set
    End Property
```

Figure 4-5. *Validation added to Set method*

This additional validation would throw an exception if the value was less than one. By adding this validation to the public property, the value is guaranteed to be in an acceptable range to be used within the Math class.

After the End Property line, add a new private function called Multiply that accepts two integer parameters called FirstNumber and SecondNumber, both of which are ByVal. The function returns an Integer result:

```
Private Function Multiply(ByVal FirstValue As Integer,
ByVal SecondValue As Integer) As Integer
End Function
```

Now you need to multiply the two parameters together and return the result. The code to do this would be

```
Return FirstValue * SecondValue
```

You may ask yourself why this method accepts two parameters for values despite the fact that there is also a public property called InValue that accepts a multiplied value. The reason is that the next step is to create a public function called MultiplyBySelf that passes the intValue variable into the Multiply private method. This way the Multiply method can be used for more than one use within the class. You might also have a public function called MultiplyBy10, for example, that takes the value from intValue and the number 10 and passes them into the Multiply private method.

Now you will create the public function called MultiplyBySelf, which doesn't have parameters but returns an integer result:

```
Public Function MultiplyBySelf() as Integer
Return Multiply(intValue,intValue)
End Function
```

The resulting code is shown in Figure 4-6.

```
Public Class Math
    Private intValue As Integer
    Public Property InValue() As Integer
        Get
            Return intValue
        End Get
        Set(ByVal value As Integer)
            If intValue > 0 Then
                intValue = value
            Else
                Throw New Exception("InValue can not be less than 1")
            End If
        End Set
    End Property
    Public Function MultiplyBySelf() As Integer
        Return Multiply(intValue, intValue)
    End Function
    Private Function Multiply(ByVal FirstValue As Integer, ByVal SecondValue As Intege
        Return FirstValue * SecondValue
    End Function
End Class
```

Figure 4-6. *Complete class code*

After you create the MultiplyBySelf method, it's time to build the Encapsulation class into an assembly that can be used by another application. To do this, click on the Build menu and then select Build Encapsulation.

Now you've created the assembly and it's ready to be used by another project. Close the Encapsulation project and create a new web site called Chapter4.

Your first task is to add a reference to the newly created assembly. This way the new ASP.NET application knows where to find the .dll file (assembly) and can use it. If you create your own assembly, then you must add a reference to any project that you create that uses that assembly. To do this, open the Solution Explorer, right-click the web site URL, and choose Add Reference as shown in Figure 4-7.

When the Add Reference window appears, click on the Browse tab, change the drive to C:, and then find the folder called Encapsulation, as shown in Figure 4-8. The Encapsulation folder was created at the same time as the project Encapsulation.

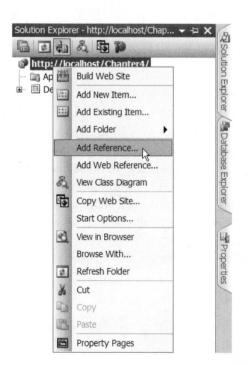

Figure 4-7. *Adding a reference*

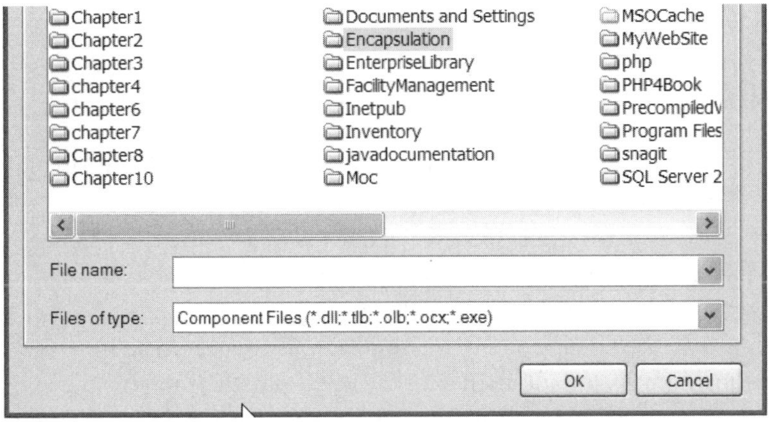

Figure 4-8. *Finding the Encapsulation folder*

Open the Encapsulation folder and then the bin/Debug folder. Click on the Encapsulation.dll file and click OK as shown in Figure 4-9.

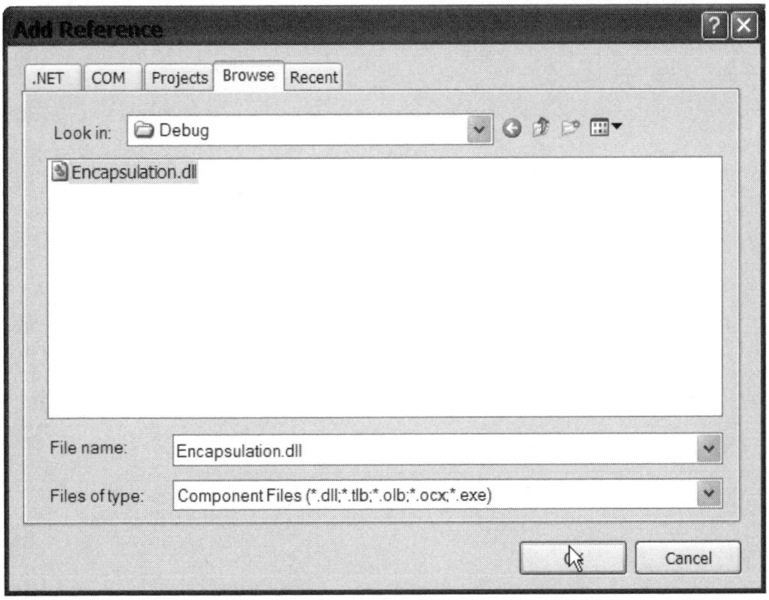

Figure 4-9. *Choosing Encapsulation.dll*

When you open the Encapsulation folder from the C: drive, you'll see a folder called bin, which you should then select. Any project that you create will hold its .dll files in the bin folder. Also, any class library or Windows application will create a single .dll file. To use that assembly (in this case Encapsulation.dll) in another project, it must be referenced in the following way. When you reference a .dll file in VS2005, it's copied to the current project's bin folder. To verify this in IIS, you will find Encapsulation.dll in the folder c:\inetpub\wwwroot\Chapter4\bin. If you create a web site without IIS, then the bin folder will be inside the folder where the project was created (probably c:\chapter4).

Now that you have referenced the Encapsulation class library, it's a good time to look at the class using the Object Browser. You'll remember that the Object Browser shows all of the properties and methods of the class. To view the Encapsulation library with the Object Browser, open the Default.aspx.vb file and then choose Object Browser from the View menu. The Encapsulation assembly will be at the top. Click the + sign next to the Encapsulation assembly and the Encapsulation namespace will appear. Click the + sign next to the Encapsulation namespace and then click the Math class. The methods and property of the Math class within the Encapsulation namespace will appear on the right as shown in Figure 4-10.

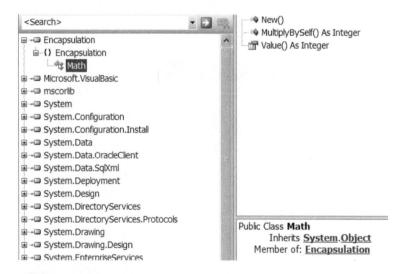

Figure 4-10. *Encapsulation assembly within the Object Browser*

Information Hiding Example

My next example will show you how information hiding does not allow the client object (in this case the ASP.NET application) to see the private Multiply method or the intValue private variable of the Math class. To start this example, double-click the Default.aspx.vb file from the Solution Explorer. You may need to click the + sign next to the Default.aspx file within the Solution Explorer in order to view it.

When the Default.vb file opens, add `Private clsMath as Encapsulation.Math` after the Inherits System.Web.UI.Page. The resulting code appears in Figure 4-11.

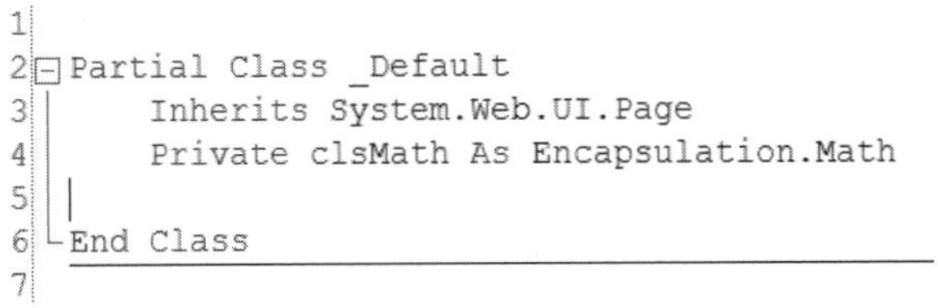

```
1
2 Partial Class _Default
3     Inherits System.Web.UI.Page
4     Private clsMath As Encapsulation.Math
5
6 End Class
7
```

Figure 4-11. *Declaring a variable of type Encapsulation.Math*

The clsMath variable is now a variable of type Encapsulation.Math class. To test your information hiding, create a private sub called Test:

```
Private Sub Test
End Sub
```

Between the previous two lines, type **clsMath**, followed by a period. This will display a list of the properties and methods of the Math class, as shown in Figure 4-12.

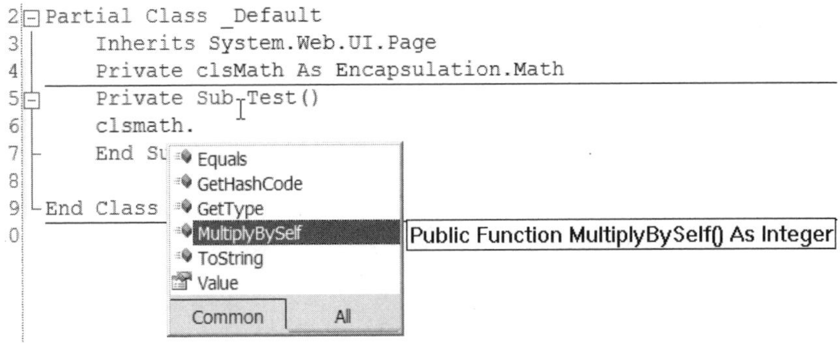

Figure 4-12. *Public properties and methods of the Encapsulation.Math class*

Notice that you don't see a method called Multiply. If you didn't create the Math class yourself, you wouldn't know that the MultiplyBySelf method doesn't really do much work other than passing the public property value to the Multiply private method. Again that is because the method Multiply is private and only used by the Math class: also called information hiding. What you *do* see here is called the interface of the class.

The *interface* of a class is made up of all the public properties and methods that are exposed to other classes when they implement the class. The interface is the mechanism that allows other developers to know which properties and methods are available from a class that you've created. Within VB.NET, an interface is also an object that can be created separately from the class. An interface provides even more separation between the communication of other classes and the actual class implementation. Check out the .NET

Framework help menu for more information on implementing interfaces, as they are out of the scope of this book.

Before moving on, delete the private sub called Test that you just created.

Encapsulation Example

My next example will show you how encapsulation can allow the implementation of the Math class to change without causing a problem with the client—as long as what the client application knows of the Math class does not change.

To get started, open the Default.aspx file from the Solution Explorer. Within the Toolbox find the TextBox control and then click and drag the control onto the Default.aspx page. Add a second TextBox control as well, so that there are two TextBox controls on the page. Also, click and drag two labels from the Toolbox to the Default.aspx surface. Make the page look like Figure 4-13 by moving the TextBox and Label controls into position.

Click on the top Label and view the Properties window. The Properties window allows you to view all exposed properties for the control that you are highlighting. (You can learn more about web forms and controls in Chapter 9.) Within the Properties window, change the Text property to Inbound and the ID property to lblInBound as shown in Figure 4-14.

Click on the TextBox control next to the Inbound label and then change the ID property to txtInbound. Next, click on the other Label, and change the Text property to Result and the ID property to lblResult.

Next, change the other TextBox control's name property to txtResult. Click and drag a button control from the Toolbox onto the Default.aspx page. Change the ID property to btnMultiply and the Text property to Multiply. When you're finished, Default.aspx should look like Figure 4-15.

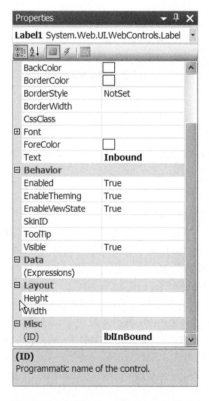

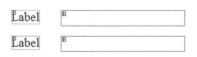

Figure 4-13. *Default.aspx with two labels and two text boxes*

Figure 4-14. *Setting the properties*

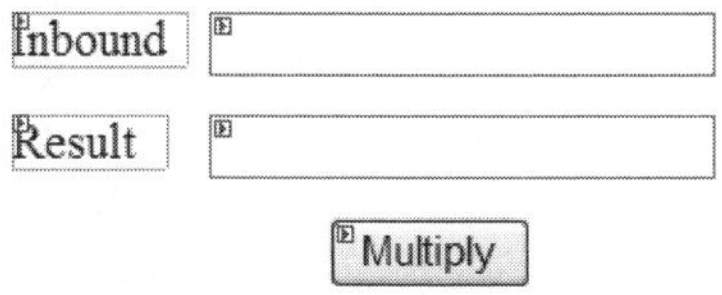

Figure 4-15. *Completed labels, text boxes, and button*

If you want something to happen when you click the Multiply button, you must write some code for the click event. To write this code, double-click the Multiply button. This will open the .aspx.vb file, create the click event, and place the cursor within this event. When you click the Multiply button, a new instance of the Math class will be created using the clsMath variable. At the same time, the value from the Inbound text box will be assigned to the Value property of the Math class instance. Next, the MultiplyBySelf method of the clsMath instance will be called and its result is placed in the Result text box:

```
clsMath = New Encapsulation.Math
clsMath.InValue = CInt(txtInbound.Text)
txtResult.Text = clsMath.MultiplyBySelf
```

Let's go through this code line by line.

The first line of code officially creates an instance of the Encapsulation.Math class. This is different from the variable declaration created earlier because it only created a variable of type Encapsulation.Math. The New keyword must be used to create a new instance of any class.

The second line of code uses the CInt built-in function of VB.Net to convert the value from the txtInbound text box to an integer and then to assign the result to the InValue property of the clsMath instance of the Encapsulation.Math class.

The third line calls the MultiplyBySelf method of the clsMath instance of the Encapsulation.Math class and assigns the result to the txtResults text box.

Now that you've completed the application, it's time to test it out. Make sure you've deleted the private sub called Test that you created in the information hiding section. Then, start the application by choosing Start Without Debugging from the Debug menu. When the Default page appears, type 4 in the Inbound text box and then click Multiply. The number 16 should appear in the result text box, as shown in Figure 4-16.

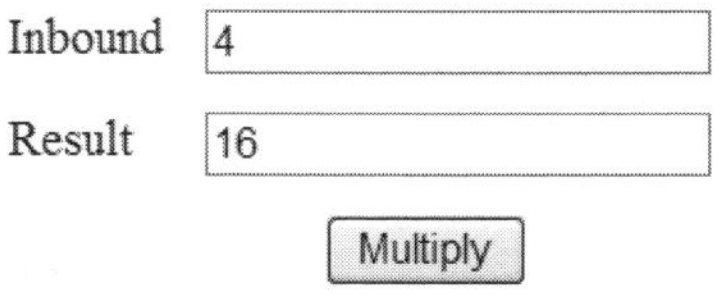

Figure 4-16. *Result of Multiply*

Changes can be made to the implementation of the encapsulated class without causing a problem with the client application. To see this, delete the reference to the Encapsulation.dll file while you have the Chapter4 project open. Go to the Solution Explorer and then delete the three encapsulation files within the bin folder. Doing this will remove the reference to the Encapsulation assembly.

Next, open the Encapsulation project again. Find the MultiplyBySelf public function within the Math.vb file. Remove the line `Return Multiply(IntValue, IntValue)` and replace it with `Return IntValue*IntValue`. Now this line will simply multiply the private variable by itself instead of passing the value to the Multiply private function, which is an example of the implementation changing. The interface to this class is still the same, but the implementation has now changed. You can now build the Encapsulation class into an assembly by clicking the Build menu and choosing Build Encapsulation.

Open the Chapter4 project again and add the reference back for the Encapsulation.dll file. After you've added the reference again, choose Start Without Debugging from the Debug menu. When the Default page appears, enter 4 as the Inbound value and then click the Multiply button. The value 16 should appear in the Result text box.

This example shows that the implementation of the encapsulated class can be changed, as long as the interface is not broken, which would cause a problem with the client.

To see how the client application can be affected by the assembly, open up the Encapsulation project. When the project opens, open the Math.vb file (if it is not already opened). Add a parameter called InValue that is defined as an integer to the MultiplyBySelf method and then change the parameters going into the Multiply method so that they use the InValue parameter instead of intvalue:

```
Public Function MultiplyBySelf(ByVal InValue As Integer) As Integer
Return Multiply(InValue, InValue)
End Function
```

After you make this change, you should build the assembly. Go back to the Chapter4 web site project and choose Start Without Debugging from the Debug menu again. Provide 4 for the Inbound value again and then click the Multiply button. The result, 16, should also come back again. You made a change to the MultiplyBySelf method interface for the Encapsulation.Math class, but the Chapter4 project has a local copy of the assembly stored within its bin folder. (This copy was made when the reference was added.) The Chapter4 web site is still working with that copy, which is why the Chapter4 web site still works. The problem comes in when a developer changes the interface like you did in MultiplyBySelf and makes other changes that require all applications using the assembly to reload the assembly.

Close the Default.aspx web page if it is still running and go to the Chapter4 project. Next, go to the Solution Explorer and delete the three files that you find there. This will remove the reference to the Encapsulation assembly. Now add the reference back in again. After the reference is added, a blue line will appear under the call `txtResult.Text = clsMath.MultiplyBySelf`. If you put your mouse over the blue line, the error will appear, as shown in Figure 4-17.

```
Protected Sub btnMultiply_Click(ByVal sender As Object, ByVal e As System.EventArg

    clsMath = New Encapsulation.Math
    clsMath.InValue = CInt(txtInbound.Text)
    txtResult.Text = clsMath.MultiplyBySelf
                     Argument not specified for parameter 'InValue' of 'Public Function MultiplyBySelf(InValue As Integer) As
End Sub            Integer'.
```

Figure 4-17. *Error after interface was broken*

The good news is that because of the way the .NET Framework and VS2005 work, your application did not break immediately as it would have in the past. Your application has its own copy of the .dll file and wasn't impacted by the change you made. However, you can see how a change to the interface or the way that an encapsulated class is implemented can have an impact on any client application that uses it.

Conclusion

In this chapter, I've provided an overview of both encapsulation and information hiding. I've also showed you how information hiding is implemented within VB.NET and encapsulation can be used to create class libraries that can be used by other applications. Finally, I showed you what can happen when the interface of an encapsulated class is changed and existing clients attempt to use it. Chapter 5 will cover the concept of inheritance and how it can extend classes and the encapsulation of classes.

■ ■ ■

CHAPTER 5

Inheritance

In this chapter, I'll introduce the concepts of inheritance, overriding, and abstract classes and how to implement them within VB.NET.

Inheritance

Inheritance within OOP is the ability for one class to copy another class but also add its own functionality. Inheritance allows you to develop one class, called the *base class*, which contains core functionality and properties, and then copy it to another class, called the *derived class*. A derived class can include new methods and properties, but its base class is left unchanged.

Inheritance is important because it allows you to copy core functionality from other classes to a new class. Without this concept, you would need to maintain all of those classes if anything changed in the core functionality. However, with inheritance you can define the core functionality in one class and then inherit the functionality from that class to make other classes. Any change to the core functionality in the base class (the one you inherited from) would automatically be reflected in the derived classes (those inheriting the base class).

One rule of thumb to use when determining if you want to use inheritance is whether an "is-a" scenario exists. Later in the book I discuss a business process for a help desk application. In that case, a user may be a general user, a technician, or a help desk manager. The core information about a user is the same, but there are additional "features" available for a technician or help desk manager. So, the technician and the help desk manager are both general users. Therefore an "is-a" relationship exists between both the technician and user and the help desk manager and user.

A payroll application can also be a real-world example of inheritance. Say you have two types of employees: salaried and hourly. Both have some information in common, such as a first and last name, date of birth, and address. However, salaried employees also have salaries and per-pay amounts, whereas hourly employees have an hourly wage and a running count of the number of hours they've worked. A salaried employee "is-an" employee and an hourly employee "is-an" employee. This means that the base class would be Employee, and two classes (Salaried and Hourly) can be derived from the base class. You would create the base class (Employee) containing the core data and functionality such as the first name, last name, date of birth, and address. Next you would create a class called SalaryEmployee that inherits the Employee class and also adds the salary and per-pay amount as properties. Then create a class called HourlyEmployee that inherits the Employee class and also adds hourly wage and the number of hours worked as properties.

Inheritance in VB.NET

Within VB.NET, all classes are inheritable by default unless marked with the NotInheritable keyword. You can inherit from other classes within a project or from classes within other applications (assemblies) that your project references (see Chapter 4 for more information on how to add a project reference).

VB.NET allows only *single inheritance*, which means a class can only inherit from one other class. You can't have a class that inherits from more than one class. To prevent exposing any private items within the base class, the scope of the class (Private, Public, and so on) of a derived class must be equal to or more restrictive than the base class. This means a public class can't inherit from a private class.

The MustInherit class scope (access modifier) can be used in the base class to specify that the class must be inherited from and can't be used directly. If a class has the MustInherit access modifier, you must derive a class from it.

To see how inheritance works in VB.NET, create a new web site called Chapter5. After you've created this project, add a new class file called Employee. Declare three private variables (strFirstName,strLastName,dteDateofBirth) and define three public properties (First Name, Last Name, Date of Birth). Finally, add a public sub called ConcatName as defined in the following code:

```
Public Class Employee
    Private strFirstName As String
    Private strLastName As String
    Private dteDateOfBirth As Date

    Public Property FirstName() As String
        Get
            Return strFirstName
        End Get
        Set(ByVal value As String)
            strFirstName = value
        End Set
    End Property
```

```
        Public Property LastName() As String
            Get
                Return strLastName
            End Get
            Set(ByVal value As String)
                strLastName = value
            End Set
        End Property
        Public Property DateOfBirth() As Date
            Get
                Return DteDateOfBirth
            End Get
            Set(ByVal value As Date)
                DteDateOfBirth = value
            End Set
        End Property
        Public Sub ConCatName(ByVal FirstName As String, ByVal LastName As String, ➡
ByRef FullName As String)
            FullName = FirstName & LastName
        End Sub


End Class
```

After you create the Employee class file, create a new class file called SalaryEmployee.vb. When you've created the SalaryEmployee class, add the following line immediately after the Public Class SalaryEmployee code:

```
Inherits Employee
```

This line of code will allow the SalaryEmployee class to inherit the existing Employee class. Your code file for SalaryEmployee.vb should look like Figure 5-1.

```
1   Imports Microsoft.VisualBasic
2
3 □ Public Class SalaryEmployee
4         Inherits Employee
5
6   └ End Class
7
```

Figure 5-1. *Inheriting the Employee class*

Tip An alternative to using the two lines is to include both the inherits and the class name on the same line, such as Public Class SalaryEmployee:Inherits Employee.

At this time, you have two classes, the original Employee class, which is your base class, and the SalaryEmployee class, which is the derived class.

To see how an inherited class works, save the SalaryEmployee class and then open the Default.aspx.vb file. Choose Page from the drop-down list at the top left of the page and then Load from the top right of the page. This will create the Page_Load sub as shown in Figure 5-2.

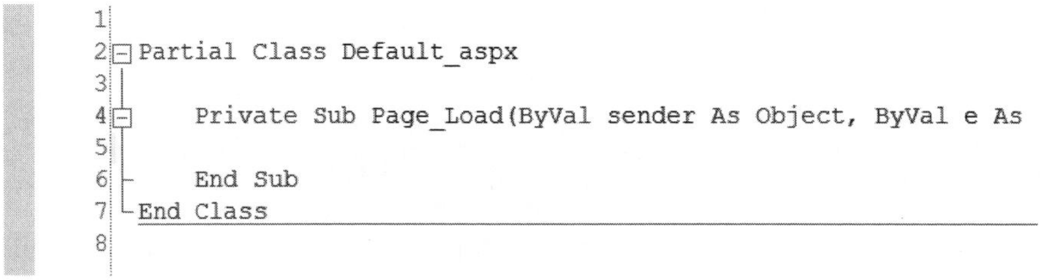

```
1
2  Partial Class Default_aspx
3
4      Private Sub Page_Load(ByVal sender As Object, ByVal e As
5
6      End Sub
7  End Class
8
```

Figure 5-2. *Revised Default.aspx.vb file*

Now declare a variable of type SalaryEmployee with the following line of code after the Private Sub Page_Load code line (place this on line 5):

```
Dim clsSalaryEmployee as SalaryEmployee
```

On the next line type **clsSalaryEmployee** followed by a period, and the IntelliSense drop-down list will appear as shown in Figure 5-3.

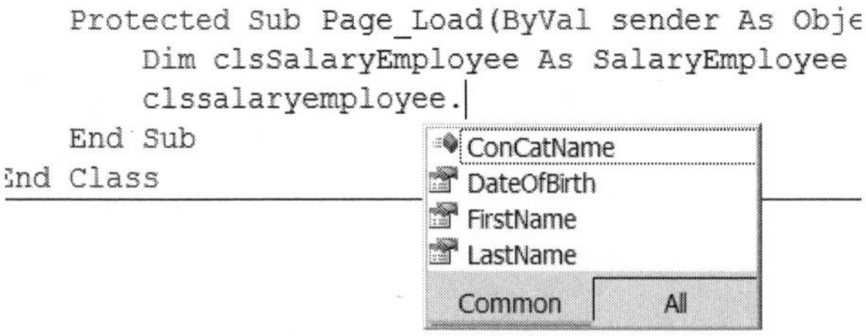

```
Protected Sub Page_Load(ByVal sender As Obje
    Dim clsSalaryEmployee As SalaryEmployee
    clssalaryemployee.|
    End Sub                    ◆ ConCatName
End Class                      📑 DateOfBirth
                               📑 FirstName
                               📑 LastName
                               
                               Common        All
```

Figure 5-3. *IntelliSense for SalaryEmployee class*

This shows you that the SalaryEmployee class did in fact inherit all of the public methods and properties of the Employee class. Now the SalaryEmployee class is an exact copy of the Employee class.

However, this will not complete the functionality that would be required for a salaried employee. Instead, this will just allow the SalaryEmployee class to have the core functionality that is required for all employees. To add the specific functionality that is needed for a salaried employee, methods and properties must be added to the SalaryEmployee class.

Open the SalaryEmployee.vb file. Add a new private variable called intSalary as an integer and then an integer public property called Salary. The SalaryEmployee.vb file should look like Figure 5-4 when you are done.

```
Imports Microsoft.VisualBasic

Public Class SalaryEmployee
    Inherits Employee
    Private intSalary As Integer
    Public Property Salary() As Integer
        Get
            Return intSalary
        End Get
        Set(ByVal value As Integer)
            intSalary = value
        End Set
    End Property
```

Figure 5-4. *Updating the SalaryEmployee class*

Return to the Default.aspx.vb file and, if you do not already have clsSalaryEmployee followed by a period within the page_load sub, add that line again so that the IntelliSense for clsSalaryEmployee is shown as in Figure 5-5.

Figure 5-5. *Revised IntelliSense for clsSalaryEmployee*

As you can see, the public property for Salary is accessible in the SalaryEmployee class. However, the Salary public property would not be available for an instance of the Employee class, since the property was only added to the derived SalaryEmployee class. To show this, create a new variable called clsEmployee as an instance of the Employee class within the Page_Load sub in the Default.aspx.vb page. The Default.aspx.vb page should look like Figure 5-6.

```
Protected Sub Page_Load(ByVal sender As Objec
    Dim clsSalaryEmployee As SalaryEmployee
    Dim clsEmployee As Employee
    |
    clssalaryemployee.
End Sub
Class
```

Figure 5-6. *Revised Default.aspx.vb file*

After the line that was used to show the interface (properties and methods) of the SalaryEmployee class (clsSalaryEmployee), add a line with just clsEmployee followed by a period. This will show the IntelliSense for clsEmployee, as shown in Figure 5-7.

```
Protected Sub Page_Load(ByVal sender As Objec
    Dim clsSalaryEmployee As SalaryEmployee
    Dim clsEmployee As Employee

    clsSalaryEmployee.
    clsEmployee.|
End Sub              ConCatName
End Class             DateOfBirth
                      FirstName
                      LastName
                      Common        All
```

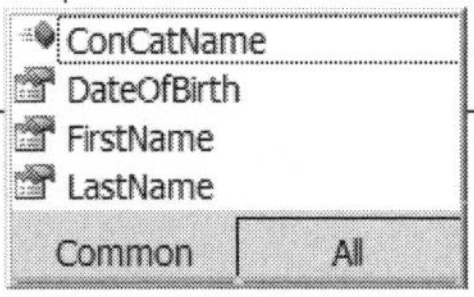

Figure 5-7. *IntelliSense for clsEmployee class*

Notice that the Salary public property is not available for the Employee class—it is only available for the SalaryEmployee class, because the public property was added to the derived class, Salaried, instead of the base class, Employee.

Overriding

A derived class inherits methods and properties from the base class. You can, however, change the behavior of a base method in the derived class by *overriding* the base method. If Object A is the base class and contains a method called DetermineBenefits, and Object B inherits from Object A, it's possible for Object B to implement its own method called DetermineBenefits and that Object B's DetermineBenefits method will be used. In general, the base class implements the default behavior for the method, and if the derived class requires special implementation details, the derived class will override the default method provided by the base class. The Overridable keyword allows a property or method to be overridden in the derived class. In the example I just gave you, Object A would need to have Overridable as part of its declaration of the DetermineBenefits method. The Overrides keyword overrides an overridable property or method from the base class.

In the example I just gave you, Object B would need to use the Overrides keyword as part of its declaration of the DetermineBenefits method. The NotOverridable keyword prevents a property or method in the base class from being overridden in the inherited class. Public methods are NotOverridable by default. The MustOverride keyword requires the derived class to override the property or method from the base class.

Continuing with the employee example used in this chapter, there is typically a difference in benefits between the hourly employee, salaried employee, and executive. So, you'll need to introduce a new class, called ExecutiveEmployee. The hourly and salaried employees in this example have their benefits determined the same way, but the benefits of the executives are determined in a different way. To implement this, a method called DetermineBenefits that is overridable will be added to the Employee class. The Employee class will provide a default implementation that will work for the salaried and hourly employees, but that will be overridden for the executive employees.

First, add a new overridable method to the employee base method. Add the following code to the Employee class:

```
Public Overridable Function DetermineBenefits() As String
Return "70% paid health care, dental insurance, life insurance"
End Function
```

Now create a new class called ExecutiveEmployee and call the file ExecutiveEmployee.vb. Next, add :Inherits Employee at the end of the class declaration so that the class declaration looks like `Public class ExecutiveEmployee:Inherits Employee`. Add the following code to the Executive class to implement the DetermineBenefits method:

```
Public Overrides Function DetermineBenefits() As String
Return "20% bonus, country club membership"
End Function
```

To demonstrate how this works, open the Default.aspx page and add a new textbox control called txtsalaried and a label called lblsalaried, with a text of salaried benefits. Next, add a button called btnsalaried, with a text of salaried. Then, add a new textbox control called txtexecutive and a label called lblexecutive, with a text of executive benefits. Finally, add a button called btnexecutive with a text of executive. The resulting page is shown in Figure 5-8.

Figure 5-8. *Completed Default.aspx page*

Double-click the Salaried button. This will open the Default.aspx.vb file and create a sub for the Salaried button's button click event. When the page opens, find the Page_Load sub that was created earlier in the chapter and delete any code fragments that might exist. Above the Page_Load sub line, and below the class declaration, add two private variables called clsSalaryEmployee and clsExecutiveEmployee. Each of these will create an instance of its respective class. The code in Default.aspx.vb should look like Figure 5-9.

```
Partial Class _Default
    Inherits System.Web.UI.Page
    Private clsSalaryEmployee As SalaryEmployee
    Private clsExecutiveEmployee As ExecutiveEmployee

    Protected Sub Page_Load(ByVal sender As Object, By

    End Sub
    Protected Sub btnSalaried_Click(ByVal sender As Ob

    End Sub

End Class
```

Figure 5-9. *Added variables*

After you've added the variables, add a line of code to the btnSalaried_Click sub to create a new instance of the SalaryEmployee class. Next, add a line to assign the value returned from the DetermineBenefits method of the salaried class to the txtsalaried text box, as shown in the this code:

```
clsSalaryEmployee = new SalaryEmployee
txtsalaried.Text = clsSalaryEmployee.DetermineBenefits
```

Now choose btnexecutive from the left drop-down list at the top of the page. After choosing btnexecutive, choose Click from the right drop-down list at the top of the page. This will create a btnexecutive_click sub. Within this newly created sub, add the following code to create an instance of the executive class and then assign the string returned from DetermineBenefits:

```
clsExecutiveEmployee= New ExecutiveEmployee
txtexecutive.Text = clsExecutiveEmployee.DetermineBenefits
```

To test this out, choose Build web site from the Build menu and then choose Start without debugging from the Debug menu. The Default.aspx page with the two labels, the two text boxes, and the two buttons will appear. Click the Salaried button. The text "70% paid health care, dental insurance, life insurance" will appear in the text box next to the

Salaried label and button. Click the Executive button. The text "20% bonus, country club membership" will appear in the text box next to the Executive label and button. This is shown in Figure 5-10.

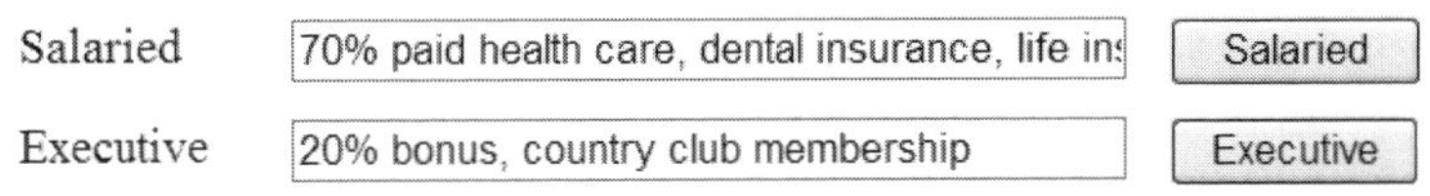

| Salaried | 70% paid health care, dental insurance, life ins | Salaried |
| Executive | 20% bonus, country club membership | Executive |

Figure 5-10. *Results of Salaried and Executive button clicks*

You can see that both classes produced the results that were expected. The SalaryEmployee class produced the text string that was in the DetermineBenefit method the salaried class inherited from the Employee class. The ExecutiveEmployee class produced the text string that was created in the DetermineBenefit method of the ExecutiveEmployee class, not the text from the Employee class, since the ExecutiveEmployee class overrode the Employee class.

This is not a completely real-world example, at least not yet. The executive does receive extra benefits such as a bonus and country club membership, but what the existing classes don't take into account is that the executive also receives the same benefits as the other employees. So the text from the DetermineBenefits base class (employee) must be added to the text defined within the DetermineBenefits method of the Executive class. To do this, you'll use the keyword *MyBase*.

The MyBase keyword is used to call a method in the base class while overriding that method in the derived class. This allows you to call the base class's method while adding more functionality to it in the derived class. MyBase refers to the immediate base class and its inherited members, but it can't be used to access private properties or methods of the base class. MyBase is a keyword, not an object, so it can't be assigned to a variable or passed to a procedure. MyBase can't be used to call methods from the base class defined as MustOverride.

To implement the complete executive benefits package, you must add the MyBase keyword to the DetermineBenefits method of the ExecutiveEmployee class. To do this, add the code & MyBase.DetermineBenefits to the DetermineBenefits method of the Executive class. The resulting implementation of the DetermineBenefits method of the Executive class will have the following code:

```
Return "20% bonus, country club membership" & MyBase.DetermineBenefits
```

To test this out, run the application again and click the Executive button. You may need to move within the text box, but you should see the salaried benefits appear along with the executive benefits. The resulting text in the Executive text box would be, "20% bonus, country club membership 70% paid health care, dental insurance, life insurance".

Abstract Classes

Abstract classes provide a simple skeleton of a class with methods and properties, but most of the methods do not actually have functionality. This creates a more generic class that can be used by others to implement functionality. In general, unlike overloading, where the base class provides a default implementation, an abstract class does not provide (or provides very little) implementation. A method or methods are declared, but they only provide a shell to be filled in when implemented by the derived class later. They are most useful when creating components, because they allow you to add functionality to some of the methods, but leave the functionality of other methods to be added later when the class is implemented for a specific reason. Abstract classes are implemented within VB.NET as classes with the MustInherit scope (access modifier). All methods defined within the abstract class must use the MustOverride key word as mentioned in the previous section. Each method must receive the same number and type of arguments and have the same return value as the overridden method in the abstract class.

To further expand on my example of the different types of employees, consider the possibility of having not just salaried employees and hourly employees but contract and part-time employees as well. For example, it's possible that the contract employees would be paid only a certain percentage of their contract for each time period (such as a month) or that their pay would be based on a percentage of the contracted work they've completed. A part-time employee may be paid on a different schedule than a full-time employee. So you see, we could have four different types of employees—maybe an abstract class that creates a basis for the general employee and then can implement its own functionality would be better.

Our Employee class from this chapter can be changed to be an abstract class. Since there are a variety of types of employees and a variety of types of ways to calculate the pay for an employee, the employee base class may provide a method called CalculatePay but provide no actual implementation. Each class that derives from the base Employee class would need to provide the implementation of the CalculatePay method based on the characteristics of that derived class.

To do this, first delete the Default.aspx file (you will need to create a new web form) and then delete executive.vb from the app_code folder. These files need to be deleted, because they implemented the executive class and the client of an override class. You are now going to make the Employee base class an abstract class, which must be inherited and can't be overridden. The two examples would get in each other's way.

Open the Employee.vb file. Next, add MustInherit between public and class in the class declaration statement, so that the line looks like `Public MustInherit Class Employee`. Also, add MustOverride before the ConcatName sub you created and used earlier in the chapter. Remove the code that exists within the ConcatName sub and the DetermineBenefits sub. The resulting sub declarations appear in Figure 5-11.

```
Imports Microsoft.VisualBasic

Public MustInherit Class Employee
    Private strFirstName As String
    Private strLastName As String
    Private dteDateOfBirth As Date

    Public MustOverride Sub ConCatName(ByVal FirstName As String,

    Public MustOverride Function DetermineBenefits() As String

    Public MustOverride Function CalculatePay() As Decimal
```

Figure 5-11. *MustOverride*

Notice that when MustOverride is present, you can't define an End Function. Since you can't define any implementation details, there is no End Function necessary.

Next open the SalaryEmployee.vb file. You will notice the SalaryEmployee class declaration has a blue squiggle line under it. That is VS2005 letting you know that the SalaryEmployee class must override all of the methods in the abstract class (Employee). Create a sub that matches the ConCatName sub, a function that matches the DetermineBenefits function, and a function that matches the CalculatePay function.

As you do this, you will notice if you enter Public Overrides followed by a space, the method names that you have not yet defined will appear as shown in Figure 5-12. Choose the name from the list and press the spacebar to have the method declaration automatically fill in.

```
Public Class SalaryEmployee
    Inherits Employee
    Private intSalary As Integer
    Public Property Salary() As Integer
        Get
            Return intSalary
        End Get
        Set(ByVal value As Integer)
            intSalary = value
        End Set
    End Property
    Public Overrides Sub ConCatName(ByVal

    End Sub
    Public overrides
                        ┌─────────────────────────────┐
                        │ ◦ CalculatePay() As Decimal  │
                        │ ◦ DetermineBenefits() As String │
                        └─────────────────────────────┘
```

Figure 5-12. *IntelliSense shows methods to override*

After you declare the CalculatePay method, enter the following line of code for the method:

```
return cdec(intsalary)/52
```

This will convert the value of the salary to a decimal value, and divide that value by 52, which is the number of weeks in a year. This determines the weekly pay for the salaried employee.

Now you should create a new class called HourlyEmployee that inherits from employee and overrides the necessary methods. The HourlyEmployee class should have a private variable called decHours that is declared as a decimal value, and a private variable called decRate that is declared as a decimal value. Finally, add two public properties to the class—one called Hours and one called Rate. The completed HourlyEmployee class code is shown in Figure 5-13. When you create the new class, the class declaration Public Class HourlyEmployee will be automatically filled in. At the end of the class declaration line add a colon (:) followed by Inherits Employee and press the spacebar. The class methods will be automatically filled in for you.

```
Imports Microsoft.VisualBasic

Public Class HourlyEmployee : Inherits Employee
    Private decHours As Decimal
    Private decRate As Decimal

    Public Property Hours ...
    Public Property Rate ...

    Public Overrides Function CalculatePay() As Decimal

    End Function

    Public Overrides Sub ConCatName(ByVal FirstName As String

    End Sub

    Public Overrides Function DetermineBenefits() As String

    End Function
End Class
```

Figure 5-13. *Completed HourlyEmployee class*

I collapsed the public properties in Figure 5-13, so that I could show you the methods more clearly. After declaring all of the variables and having the methods created, add the line

```
Return decHours * decRate
```

to the CalculatePay method. This will calculate the pay for an hourly employee by multiplying the employee's hours worked by their hourly rate.

Now you've implemented a way to calculate the pay for both the SalaryEmployee class and the HourlyEmployee class. To see how this works, first create a new web form called Calculate.aspx. Next, add a new text box to the Calculate.aspx page called txtCalculateSalary, with a label called lblCalculateSalary and a text property of Calculate Salary. Next, add a text box called txtSalary along with a label called lblSalary and a text property of Salary. Also, add a text box called txtHours along with a label called lblHours with a text property of Hours. Next, add a text box called txtRate along with a label called lblRate and a text property of Rate. Add a text box called txtCalculateHourly with a label called lblCalculateHourly and a text property of Calculate Hourly. Finally, add a button called btnCalculate with a text of Calculate. The resulting page should look like Figure 5-14.

Double-click the Calculate button, which will take you to the Calculate.aspx.vb file, and then create a btncalculate_click sub. Enter the following code in the btncalculate_click sub:

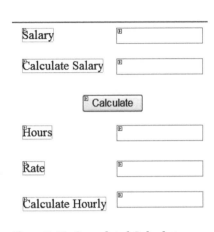

Figure 5-14. *Completed Calculate.aspx*

```
Dim clsSalaried = SalaryEmployee
Dim clsHourly = HourlyEmployee
clsSalaried = New SalaryEmployee
clsHourly = New HourlyEmployee

clsSalaried.Salary = txtSalary.text
txtcalculatesalary.Text = clsSalaried.CalculatePay.ToString

clsHourly.Rate = CDec(Trim(txtrate.Text))
clsHourly.Hours = CDec(Trim(txthours.Text))

txtcalculatehourly.Text = clsHourly.CalculatePay.ToString
```

This code will allow you to calculate the pay for both a salaried employee (salary divided by 52) and hourly (hours × rate). The first four lines of the code declare the necessary variables and create instances of the correct classes. The next two lines assign the value provided as the salary in txtsalary to the SalaryEmployee class, along with calculating the salary. The final three lines assign the rate and hours, as well as a calculation of the hourly pay.

To test this out, you may first have to set the Calculate.aspx page as the start page. To do this, right-click the Calculate.aspx page within the Solution Explorer, and choose Set

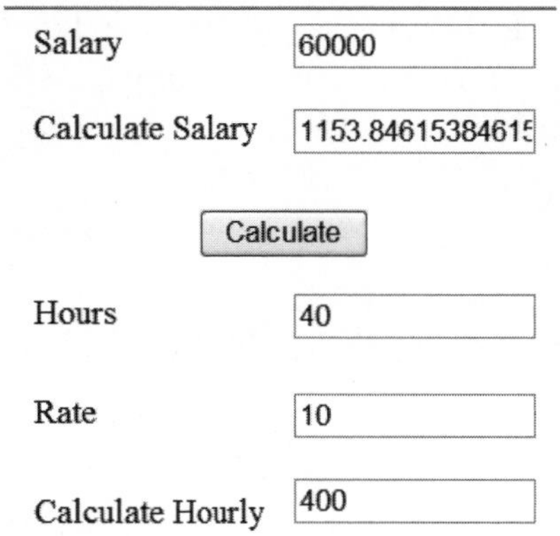

Salary   60000

Calculate Salary   1153.84615384615

Calculate

Hours   40

Rate   10

Calculate Hourly   400

Figure 5-15. *Results*

as Start Page. When the application starts, the calculate.aspx page will be the one to appear. Click Debug and then Start without debugging to view the page. Next, type a salary amount in the box next to the label Salary. My example shows 60,000. Next, enter values in the boxes next to the labels Hours and Rate. I entered 40 for the hours and 10 for the rate. Click the Calculate button. My results are shown in Figure 5-15.

You can verify these results with a calculator, but you will find that they are correct. This example has shown you how one abstract class with only method declarations can be used by the client to implement different functionality in different derived classes.

Conclusion

In this chapter, I've provided a definition of inheritance as well as an example of how inheritance is implemented within VB.NET. I gave you some information about overriding, and presented an example of how it could be used in a common business process. I also discussed abstract classes and how you can implement them.

Namespaces

In this chapter I'll cover the definition of a namespace within the .NET Framework and how to create a namespace.

The Purpose of a Namespace

A *namespace* has several different purposes. First, a namespace organizes the objects that are defined within an assembly. Remember that an assembly is made up of a class. By default, every executable file you create contains a namespace with the same name as the project that was used to create it.

Second, a class library is also a namespace. When you choose to create a class library, you create a namespace. That namespace can then have many classes within it. In this way, a namespace can be used to organize common functionality. For example, my company has a namespace that contains all of the classes that are common to the applications that we build (more on this later in this chapter).

A third purpose of a namespace is to avoid naming conflicts. Namespaces are not an OOP concept, but instead are a logical way to organize classes in a meaningful way developed for the .NET Framework.

.NET Framework Class Library

The best way to learn about namespaces and their uses is to look at the .NET Framework Class Library. The VS2005 Object Browser was introduced in Chapter 2 and will be further used in this chapter to explain the use of namespaces.

To access the Object Browser, choose View then Object Browser, as shown in Figure 6-1. The Object Browser will appear in the middle of the screen.

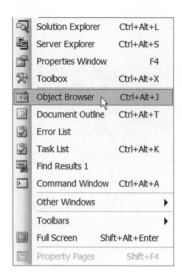

Solution Explorer	Ctrl+Alt+L
Server Explorer	Ctrl+Alt+S
Properties Window	F4
Toolbox	Ctrl+Alt+X
Object Browser	Ctrl+Alt+J
Document Outline	Ctrl+Alt+T
Error List	
Task List	Ctrl+Alt+K
Find Results 1	
Command Window	Ctrl+Alt+A
Other Windows	▶
Toolbars	▶
Full Screen	Shift+Alt+Enter
Property Pages	Shift+F4

Figure 6-1. *Choosing Object Browser from the View Menu*

Assembly **System**
    C:\WINDOWS\Microsoft.NET\Framework
\v2.0.40607\System.dll

Attributes:
[System.Reflection.AssemblyFileVersionAttribute
("2.0.40607.16"),
System.Reflection.AssemblyProductAttribute("Microsoft
(R) .NET Framework"),
System.Reflection.AssemblyCompanyAttribute
("Microsoft Corporation"),
System.Reflection.AssemblyInformationalVersionAttrib
ute("2.0.40607.16"),
System.Reflection.AssemblyCopyrightAttribute

Figure 6-2. *Information about the System namespace*

The first screen of the Object Browser will show all of the assemblies within the .NET Class Library. Each of these assemblies contains both namespaces and classes, and may well include other namespaces and the classes associated with those namespaces. If you click on one of the assemblies, additional information will appear at the bottom right of the screen. This is shown for the System namespace in Figure 6-2.

In this example, the first line tells what the assembly's name is (System) and where the file for the assembly is located, in this case the system.dll file. Below the assembly name and location is other information about the assembly.

If you click on the System assembly and expand it, as shown in Figure 6-3, you will see a list of more namespaces. In this case, the System namespace has several other namespaces within it. Namespaces found within other namespaces are called *nested namespaces*. In Figure 6-3, all of the namespaces shown are nested namespaces of the System namespace.

Within the Object Browser, there is a common technique for distinguishing namespaces from classes, methods, and properties. Each type should display differently, and you should become familiar with this technique so that you will know if a type you are looking at is a namespace, class, or something else. Notice, for example, the {} next to the namespace in Figure 6-3. You'll see that there's also a rectangle icon next to the highlighted System in Figure 6-3 that represents an assembly or .dll file. There is an assembly called System (System.dll), which contains all of the items nested under the System assembly in the Object Browser (shown in Figure 6-3).

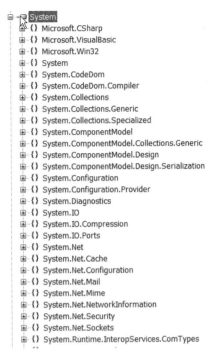

Figure 6-3. *Namespaces within the System namespace*

Within the System assembly, you will notice namespaces such as Win32, CSharp, and VisualBasic. If you expand the VisualBasic namespace, as shown in Figure 6-4, you will notice there is a class named VBCodeProvider within that namespace. This is the only class within this namespace. The icon next to the VBCodeProvider class represents a class. If you see this icon next to an item within the Object Browser, the item is a class.

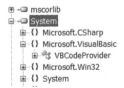

Figure 6-4. *VBCodeProvider class within the Microsoft VisualBasic namespace*

If you click on the VBCodeProvider class, you will see a list of the methods and properties appear in the top right of the Object Browser, as shown in Figure 6-5.

The methods in the list have a small block icon next to them and the properties have what looks like a card with a hand icon next to them.

```
GenerateCodeFromMember(System.CodeDom.CodeTypeMember, System.IO.TextWriter, Sys
New()
CreateCompiler() As System.CodeDom.Compiler.ICodeCompiler
CreateGenerator() As System.CodeDom.Compiler.ICodeGenerator
GetConverter(System.Type) As System.ComponentModel.TypeConverter
FileExtension() As String
LanguageOptions() As System.CodeDom.Compiler.LanguageOptions
```

Figure 6-5. *Methods and properties of the VBCodeProvider class*

If you collapse both the System namespace and System assembly (so that you are back to the top-level assembly view), you will see the other assemblies that make up the .NET Framework, as shown in Figure 6-6.

```
Microsoft.VisualBasic
mscorlib
System
System.Configuration
System.Configuration.Install
System.Data
System.Data.OracleClient
System.Data.SqlXml
System.Deployment
System.Design
System.DirectoryServices
System.DirectoryServices.Protocols
System.Drawing
System.Drawing.Design
System.EnterpriseServices
```

Figure 6-6. *Assemblies within the .NET Class Library*

Click the + sign next to System.Web. This is the assembly that contains all of the namespaces and classes that can be used for an ASP.NET application. You will notice a namespace called System.Web.UI in that list. If you click the + next to it, you will see a list of classes. These are the classes that make up the System.Web.UI namespace and that can be used to help build your ASP.NET application. You will also notice a class called *Control*. The Control class is the base class that all ASP.NET web form controls are derived from. Even further down the list is the Page class. This is the class that represents a web form and performs the request and response necessary for a web page to display.

Creating a Namespace

You can create your own namespace to provide better organization for your classes. For example, you might create a namespace named after your company, which might contain the classes with all of the reusable functionality for your company. This may include data access classes, exception classes, and others. Creating this namespace can be very useful for your company, because it would provide all your developers with common functionality. Once a namespace is coded and an assembly created, the assembly can be distributed to all developers and used with all applications. Any changes that need to be made to any of the functionality would need to be made within this namespace and then redistributed.

To begin creating a namespace, create a new class library project. Click File, then New Project. When the New Project window appears, choose Class Library, enter Chapter6 as the project name, and then c:\chapter6 as the location, as shown in Figure 6-7.

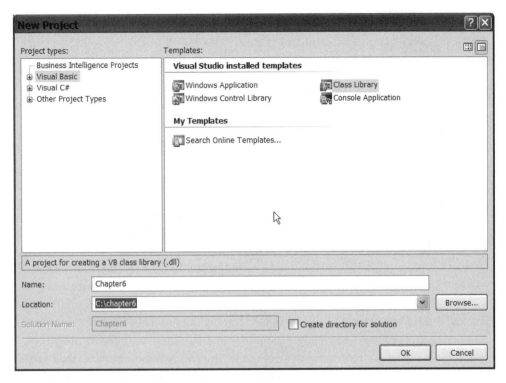

Figure 6-7. *Adding a new project called Chapter6*

This class library will now become a namespace, which means that it can contain multiple classes that provide common functionality to be used by your company. To create this class library as a namespace, you don't really need to do anything. By default, you could build this class library project into an assembly (called Chapter6) and Chapter6 would become your namespace. For our example, though, the namespace is going to be changed to MyCompany. You can change the root namespace (the base namespace for all files within the project) by clicking the My Project folder within the Solution Explorer. The Project Properties window will then appear. Find the Root Namespace textbox within the properties window and then enter MyCompany, so that will become the namespace for this assembly.

After you've changed the Root Namespace, close the Project Properties window. Next, rename the class (.vb) file that was created with the new project to Math.vb. Then add a class called UserAuth by right-clicking the project name (Chapter6) at the top of the Solution Explorer and then choosing Add and then Class, as shown in Figure 6-8.

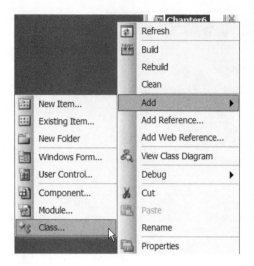

Figure 6-8. *Adding a class*

When the Add Item window appears, make sure class is already selected and enter UserAuth.vb as the file name.

Now there are two classes within the namespace. I'm going to revert to some of the prior examples and add a couple of methods and properties to the Math class and then to the User Auth class (UserAuth.vb). Then, I'll create an ASP.NET application to use these two classes.

To do this, you should first create a public function called AddIntegers that returns an integer with two integer parameters: firstInteger and secondInteger. Within the new function, return the value of the firstInteger parameter added to the secondInteger parameter. Then, create a public function called MultiplyIntegers that returns an integer with two integer parameters, firstInteger and secondInteger. Within the new function, return the value of the firstInteger parameter multiplied by the secondInteger parameter. Next, add a new function called AddDecimal that returns a decimal with two decimal parameters: firstDecimal and secondDecimal. Within the new function, return the value of the firstDecimal parameter added to the secondDecimal parameter. Finally, create a new function called MultiplyDecimal that returns a decimal with two decimal parameters, firstDecimal and secondDecimal. Within the new function, now return the value of the firstDecimal parameter multiplied by the secondDecimal parameter. Your resulting code should look like this:

```
Public Function AddIntegers(ByVal firstInteger As Integer,
ByVal secondInteger As Integer) As Integer
Return firstInteger + secondInteger
End Function


Public Function MultiplyIntegers(ByVal firstInteger As Integer,
ByVal secondInteger As Integer) As Integer
Return firstInteger * secondInteger
End Function


Public Function AddDecimal(ByVal firstDecimal As Decimal,
ByVal secondDecimal As Decimal) As Decimal
Return firstDecimal + secondDecimal
End Function
```

```
Public Function MultiplyDecimal(ByVal firstDecimal As Decimal,
ByVal secondDecimal As Decimal) As Decimal
Return firstDecimal * secondDecimal
End Function
```

Next open the UserAuth.vb file. Create a new public function called IsUserAdmin, which will return a Boolean and accept a string parameter called UserName. Within this function, add code to determine if the username parameter is equal to "Mickey," (or some other character that might be *your* favorite) and if it is, return true; otherwise, return false. The point is that eventually we will pass in your true user name and this function will return false. Create a new public function called IsUserValid that returns a Boolean and accepts a string parameter called UserName. Within this function add code to determine whether the username parameter is equal to "Mickey" or your favorite character (the same as the IsUserAdmin function) and if it is, return true; otherwise, return false. The resulting code should look like:

```
Public Function IsUserAdmin(ByVal UserName As String) As Boolean
If UserName = "Mickey" Then
Return True
Else
Return False
End If
End Function

Public Function IsUserValid(ByVal UserName As String) As Boolean
If UserName = "Mickey" Then
Return True
Else
Return False
End If
End Function
```

Now that both classes have methods, build the class library into an assembly by choosing Build Chapter6 from the Build menu. Close the class library project and then create a new web site called Chapter6.

Drag a label control onto Default.aspx, and then set the text property to First and the ID property to lblfirst. Drag a second label onto Default.aspx and set the text property to Second and the ID property to lblsecond. Finally, drag a third label onto Default.aspx and set the text property to Answer and the ID property to lblAnswer.

Drag three text box controls onto Default.aspx. The first text box has an ID property of txtfirst, the second's ID property is txtSecond, and the third's ID property is txtAnswer. Add a button control with an ID property of btnAddIntegers, a text property of Add Integers, and then a button control with an ID property of btnMultiplyIntegers with a text property of Multiply Integers. Next, add a button control with an ID property of btnAddDecimals, a text property of Add Decimals, and then a button control with an ID property of btnMultiplyDecimals with a text property of Multiply Decimals. The resulting Default.aspx should look like Figure 6-9.

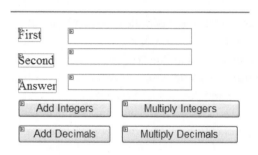

Figure 6-9. *Completed Default.aspx form*

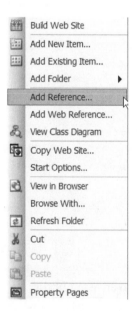

Figure 6-10. *Adding a Reference*

To use a namespace or class library, you need to reference it. To reference a namespace, you need to reference the assembly that it belongs to, in this case Chapter6.dll. Right-click the project URL at the top of the Solution Explorer (probably `http://localhost/Chapter6/`) and choose Add Reference, as shown in Figure 6-10.

The Add Reference window will now appear. Click the Browse tab to find the .dll file that you want to reference. Navigate the Look In drop-down list to the folder where the Chapter6 class library project was created (probably c:\chapter6). Open the bin folder and then the Debug folder. Chapter6.dll should be in this folder—select it and then click OK. Now there is a relationship established between the Chapter6 ASP.NET application and the chapter6.dll class library.

Right-click the Default.aspx page and choose View Code. This will show you the Default.aspx.vb file.

To show that namespaces are a good way to organize classes and allow you to create two classes with the same name within different namespaces, try declaring a private variable with

```
Private clsMath as Math
```

Remember, Math is the name of one of the classes within the MyCompany namespace. Next, create a private sub called TestClass. Within that private sub, type **clsMath** followed by a period. IntelliSense will now show you the items that make up the Math class, as shown in Figure 6-11.

Notice that the items available in the Math class (declared as clsMath) are not the same items you created earlier in the Mycompany.Math class. To determine which namespace the Math class is part of, right-click Math in the declaration of the variable (`Private clsMath as Math`) and choose Go To Definition. This will open the Object Browser and show you a definition of the class, as shown in Figure 6-12.

Remember, this is *not* the Math class that was created in the MyCompany namespace. I'll talk more about this subject after the next section.

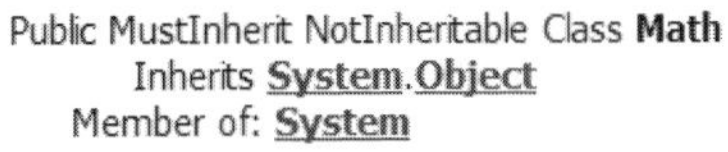

There are two ways to use the referenced namespace. First, you can type the name of the namespace, followed by the class, method, or property, such as `MyCompany.Math.AddIntegers`.

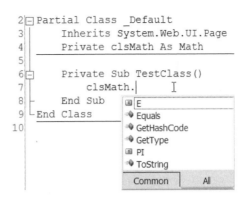

Figure 6-11. *Items available in the Math class*

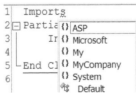

Figure 6-12. *Definition of System.Math class*

This option takes more time to code, because you always need to include the method, property, and class, as well as the namespace. A possible shortcut is to add an *Imports statement*. The Imports statement lets the compiler know that this class includes or should use the following class or namespace. An Imports statement must be at the top of the code page and a given code page can have multiple Imports statements. To use Imports on the MyCompany namespace, type **Imports**, followed by a space, on the very top line of the Default.aspx.vb file. IntelliSense will provide a list of referenced namespaces, as shown in Figure 6-13.

All of the namespaces, other than MyCompany, are referenced by default when a new web site is created. This means that you do not need to specifically import these. Choose MyCompany from the list. Now, remove the period following clsMath within the TestClass sub. Type the period again, so that the IntelliSense will appear again. This time you will notice that the methods that you added to the MyCompany.Math class now appear, as shown in Figure 6-14.

Figure 6-13. *IntelliSense provides list of namespaces.*

```
Imports MyCompany
Partial Class _Default
    Inherits System.Web.UI.Page
    Private clsMath As Math


    Private Sub TestClass()
        clsMath.
    End Sub
End Class
```

| AddDecimal |
| AddIntegers |
| Equals |
| GetHashCode |
| GetType |
| MultiplyDecimal |
| MultiplyIntegers |
| ToString |

| Common | All |

Figure 6-14. *MyCompany.Math methods*

Public Class **Math**
    Inherits **System.Object**
    Member of: **MyCompany**

Figure 6-15. *Definition of MyCompany.Math class*

Now you've seen that the namespace can be used as an organizational tool to allow you to create classes with the same name as classes that already exist within other namespaces. Right-click on the Math part of the variable declaration (Private clsMath as Math) and choose Go To Definition. This brings up the Object Browser again, and shows the information for the Math class as shown in Figure 6-15.

Since you can see that the correct class is referenced from the correct namespace, close the Object Browser if it is still open, and delete the TestClass sub. It is not needed.

Now, it's time for you to see that the classes within the namespace can be used like any other class. From the left drop-down list, on top of the code window, choose btnAddIntegers. From the right drop-down list on the top of the code window, choose Click. This will create a sub called btnAddIntegers_Click, which will handle the click event of the button btnAddIntegers. When the add integers button is clicked, the two integers in the text boxes should be passed to the AddIntegers method of the Math class and the result should be placed in the txtAnswer text box. Use the following code to accomplish this:

```
clsMath = New Math
txtAnswer.Text = clsMath.AddIntegers(txtfirst.Text, txtsecond.Text)
```

First   4

Second   5

Answer   9

| Add Integers | Multiply Integers |
| Add Decimals | Multiply Decimals |

Figure 6-16. *Results*

To test this out, start the web application by choosing Start without Debugging from the Debug menu. Type 4 for First, type **5** for Second, and then click the Add Integers button. The answer 9 should appear in the answer text box, as shown in Figure 6-16.

You can add the same code to the other click events for your other buttons. The resulting code within Default.aspx.vb would look like this:

```
Protected Sub btnAddIntegers_Click(ByVal sender As Object,
ByVal e As System.EventArgs) Handles btnAddIntegers.Click
clsMath = New Math
txtAnswer.Text = clsMath.AddIntegers(txtfirst.Text, txtsecond.Text)
End Sub

Protected Sub btnAddDecimals_Click(ByVal sender As Object,
ByVal e As System.EventArgs) Handles btnAddDecimals.Click
clsMath = New Math
txtAnswer.Text = clsMath.AddDecimal(txtfirst.Text, txtsecond.Text)
End Sub

Protected Sub btnMultiplyDecimals_Click(ByVal sender As Object,
ByVal e As System.EventArgs) Handles btnMultiplyDecimals.Click
clsMath = New Math
txtAnswer.Text = clsMath.MultiplyDecimal(txtfirst.Text, txtsecond.Text)
End Sub

Protected Sub btnMultiplyIntegers_Click(ByVal sender As Object,
ByVal e As System.EventArgs) Handles btnMultiplyIntegers.Click
clsMath = New Math
txtAnswer.Text = clsMath.AddIntegers(txtfirst.Text, txtsecond.Text)
End Sub
```

As mentioned before, a particular namespace can have another namespace within it, called a nested namespace. To create a nested namespace, open the Chapter6 class library project again. The class library will use MyCompany as a namespace. Now you are going to add a new namespace. To make this a little more meaningful to you, change the name of the Math.vb class to Integers.vb. You'll see that this will also change the name of the class. Next, add a new class called Decimals. Move the two functions (AddDecimals and MultiplyDecimals) to the Decimals class. Now you have two classes, one called Integers and one called Decimals. At the top of each of the two classes, type Namespace Math. At the end of each class file, type End Namespace. This will create a namespace called Math with two classes: Integers and Decimals. The Math namespace is already within the MyCompany namespace. The resulting code for the Integers class is

```
Namespace Math
Public Class Integers
Public Function AddIntegers(ByVal firstInteger As Integer,
ByVal secondInteger As Integer) As Integer
Return firstInteger + secondInteger
End Function
```

```
Public Function MultiplyIntegers(ByVal firstInteger As Integer,
 ByVal secondInteger As Integer) As Integer
Return firstInteger * secondInteger
End Function
End Class
End Namespace
```

The resulting code for the Decimals class is

```
Namespace Math
Public Class Decimals
Public Function AddDecimal(ByVal firstDecimal As Decimal,
ByVal secondDecimal As Decimal) As Decimal
Return firstDecimal + secondDecimal
End Function

Public Function MultiplyDecimal(ByVal firstDecimal As Decimal,
ByVal secondDecimal As Decimal) As Decimal
Return firstDecimal * secondDecimal
End Function
End Class
End Namespace
```

One useful way to view your namespace and the classes within it is to use the Class View. You can access this by choosing Class View from the View menu at the top of VS2005. The Class View will show both the namespace and the classes, as shown in Figure 6-17.

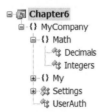

Figure 6-17. *Class View of the namespace*

Next, build the Chapter6 class library again. You'll need to go back to the Chapter6 web site project, delete the references and then add them again. To delete the references, go to the Solution Explorer and expand the bin folder. Delete the three files that are there. Then, add the reference again, as discussed earlier in the chapter. After you've added the reference again, you will notice that the code on your Default.aspx.vb page looks different. The Math class declaration will have a blue squiggle line under it. If you mouse over that blue line, you will get a pop-up message that says Type Expected. This is because MyCompany.Math is now a namespace instead of a class.

To correct this problem, find the Imports statement at the top of the code page. Type another period after Imports MyCompany. You will now see a Math namespace, as shown in Figure 6-18.

To correct the remaining issues with Default.aspx.vb, you will need to remove the clsMath declaration and replace it with two private variable declarations. The first, called clsIntegers, will be of the type Inte-

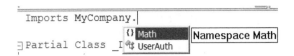

Figure 6-18. *MyCompany.Math namespace*

gers; and the second, called clsDecimals, will be of the type Decimals. Within each sub, make the necessary changes so that the manipulation of integer values is done by the Integers class and the manipulation of the decimal values is done by the Decimals class. The resulting code should look like this:

```
Private clsIntegers As Integers
Private clsDecimals As Decimals

Protected Sub btnAddIntegers_Click(ByVal sender As Object,
ByVal e As System.EventArgs) Handles btnAddIntegers.Click
clsIntegers = New Integers
txtAnswer.Text = clsIntegers.AddIntegers(txtfirst.Text, txtsecond.Text)
End Sub

Protected Sub btnAddDecimals_Click(ByVal sender As Object,
ByVal e As System.EventArgs) Handles btnAddDecimals.Click
clsDecimals = New Decimals
txtAnswer.Text = clsDecimals.AddDecimal(txtfirst.Text, txtsecond.Text)
End Sub

Protected Sub btnMultiplyDecimals_Click(ByVal sender As Object,
ByVal e As System.EventArgs) Handles btnMultiplyDecimals.Click
clsDecimals = New Decimals
txtAnswer.Text = clsDecimals.MultiplyDecimal(txtfirst.Text, txtsecond.Text)
End Sub

Protected Sub btnMultiplyIntegers_Click(ByVal sender As Object,
ByVal e As System.EventArgs) Handles btnMultiplyIntegers.Click
clsIntegers = New Integers
txtAnswer.Text = clsIntegers.AddIntegers(txtfirst.Text, txtsecond.Text)
End Sub
```

This example showed how nested namespaces work and how they can be created.

The My Namespace

The My namespace is a new namespace for VB 2005. You can use My within code to access several useful classes and features without importing or accessing the specific namespaces. These useful classes are application, computer, resources, user, and web services. The application class allows you to access some information about the application. The computer class lets you access information about the computer the application is being run on. The resources class allows you to set the culture of the application. User class allows you to get the identity of the user, if you are using Windows NT logins for your application. Finally, the web services class allows you to access and use web services. Not all of the classes are available for all of the different types of applications. For example, the application class and forms class are only available for Windows-based applications.

A good use of the My namespace within an ASP.NET application is to use the My namespace to get the login name (including the domain) of the currently logged-in user. This information can be very useful within your application. The first thing you need to do is to set up the virtual directory to use Windows Domain Authentication. If you have IIS installed, you can do this by opening the Internet Information Services administration tool from within the Administration Tools area of the control panel. First, right-click the virtual directory for the web site that you are working on (in this case Chapter6) and choose Properties. When the Properties window appears, click the Directory Security tab. On the Directory Security tab, click the Edit button at the top. If the Anonymous checkbox is checked, uncheck and verify the Integrated Windows authentication checkbox is checked, as shown in Figure 6-19.

If the anonymous access checkbox is checked, the name of the domain user cannot be found even if the Integrated Windows Authentication is checked. If Anonymous access is left checked, all users are granted access regardless of their Windows credentials. After verifying that Integrated Windows authentication is the only box checked, click the OK button.

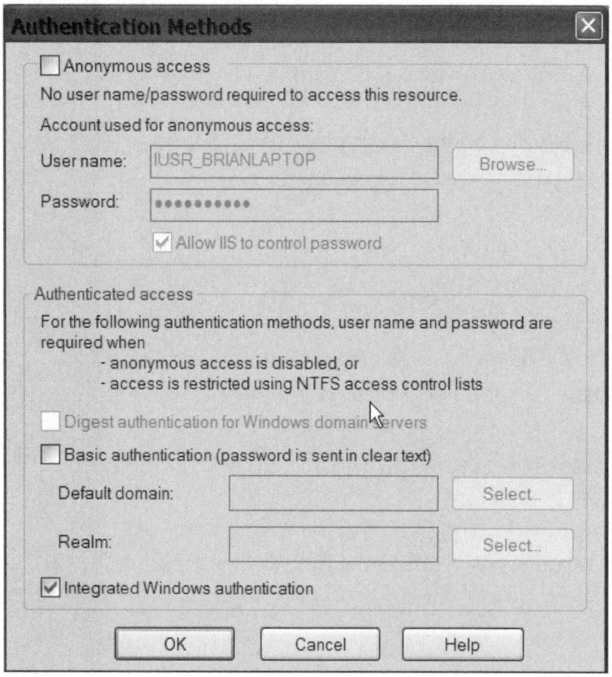

Figure 6-19. *Authentication methods*

Open the Default.aspx page and drag a label onto the form. Give it an ID property of lbllogin and leave the text property blank. Now open the Default.aspx.vb file. From the top left drop-down box choose Page Events, then from the top right drop-down box choose Load. This will create the Page_Load sub within the Default.aspx.vb file. Add:

```
lbllogin.text = "Login: " & My.User.Name
```

to the Page_Load sub.

Start the web application and you should see the name of the currently logged-in user appear within the label that was just added, as shown in Figure 6-20.

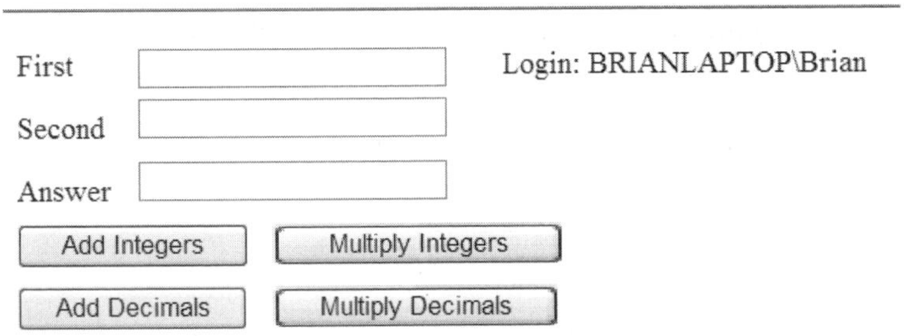

First		Login: BRIANLAPTOP\Brian
Second		
Answer		

Add Integers   Multiply Integers

Add Decimals   Multiply Decimals

Figure 6-20. *The login name appears.*

This example shows you how to get and use the name property of the User class within the My namespace. Now you can use this value to determine if the user is an administrator using the UserAuth class within the MyCompany namespace. Drag another label onto the Default.aspx page with an ID property of lblAdmin and with no value in the Text property. Open the Default.aspx.vb code page again, and then add a new declaration at the top:

```
Private clsauth as MyCompany.UserAuth
```

This will create an instance of the UserAuth class from within the MyCompany namespace and call that instance clsauth. Change the code with the Page_Load sub to be:

```
Dim strLogin As String
Dim intBegin As Integer
intBegin = InStr(My.User.Name, "\") + 1
strLogin = Mid(My.User.Name, intBegin)
lbllogin.Text = "Login: " & strLogin
clsAuth = New MyCompany.UserAuth
lbladmin.Text = "Admin: " & clsAuth.IsUserAdmin(strLogin)
```

As you probably noticed from the previous example, the Name property of the User class provides both the domain name and the user name. This set of code will determine both where the domain name ends and where the user name begins, and it will only display the user name. The first two lines of code declare variables that are local to the Page_Load sub. The first (strLogin) will hold the login name, while the second (intBegin) will be used to determine where the domain name ends and the login name begins. The third line of code uses the built-in InStr function to determine if the string "\" is contained within the name property of the User class. A value of 1 is added to that number and assigned to intBegin. intBegin then has the position of the first character of the user name (not the domain name). The next line uses the built-in function Mid to extract the characters from the name property of the User class, starting from the position represented by intBegin. The next line sets the text for the lbllogin control. The sixth line creates a new instance of the UserAuth class within the MyCompany namespace. The final line calls the IsUserAdmin method of the UserAuth class within the MyCompany namespace and passes the user name to determine if the user is an admin or not.

After the code is in place, start the application. The results should look similar to Figure 6-21, but with your currently logged in user name and False.

First   [   ]   Login: Brian

Second   [   ]   Admin: False

Answer   [   ]

[Add Integers]   [Multiply Integers]

[Add Decimals]   [Multiply Decimals]

Figure 6-21. *Completed form*

This example showed you how to get solely the name of the currently logged-in user by skipping over the domain name. There are more uses for the My namespace within ASP.NET applications; however, if you are writing applications for intranet sites, the User class within the My namespace will be very useful. You can look up more about the My namespace by searching for My within the MSDN help file.

Conclusion

In this chapter I've discussed namespaces in depth. Though namespaces aren't an OOP concept, they still provide a useful way to organize classes of functionality when using VS2005. In Chapter 7, I'll cover how to design classes based on business processes.

■ ■ ■

CHAPTER 7

Class Design

In the first part of this chapter, I'll cover how to design classes for an application based on a business process. In the second part of this chapter, I'll cover how to create the classes and then use those classes to lay the groundwork for an ASP.NET web site. The next chapter will cover designing and building web forms, which uses the classes you create in this chapter to build the web site.

Class Design Process

Class design is the process used to transform the written business processes for an application into one or more classes that will be used to implement the application. The input into this process is an overview of both the application and the business process the application will facilitate. The output will be code structures for all classes that will be used for the application.

The class design process is comprised of six steps:

1. Define the business process

2. Review the business process

3. Break down the business process

4. Create the class or classes

5. Define the properties and methods of the class or classes

6. Create the class structure

Case Study

To best illustrate the class design process, I have developed a case study based on a real-world application. This case study will explain each step in the class design process and also apply each step to the real-world application. The case study I've chosen is based on a help desk system. But it's important to note that the application that you will build over this chapter and the next will not be feature complete. This is because, as this is an introductory book, I don't want to go into the use of ADO.NET, which is used to connect to a database. Instead, for the purposes of this book, some of the methods will be hard-coded to show the concept. And later, when you are learning about ADO.NET, you can use this application to write your first ADO.NET code. What follows next is the business process overview provided as the first input into the class design process.

Business Process Overview

Your company needs a help desk system. The help desk system should allow users to create new help desk tickets and then send them to the help desk technicians to be reviewed and worked on. The user should be able to choose from a list of categories for the ticket. The user must also provide their login, their first and last names, their phone number, their location, e-mail address, a category for the ticket, and a description of the problem. The ticket itself must record the date created, the login that created the ticket, the date assigned, and the date closed. After the ticket is created (with a status of *new*), a technician at the appropriate location must be able to view the ticket. The technician should then be able to choose a level of importance for the ticket (high, medium, or low) and add any additional comments. The technician will then assign the ticket to herself and begin work on the ticket. When the work is completed the technician should be able to change the status to resolved, provide a resolution, and record her total number of minutes spent on the ticket. The user should then be able to either close the ticket or say the ticket is not resolved, depending on the situation. If a technician is waiting for parts or other support, the status can be set to pending.

Technicians must be able to see a list of the new tickets for their location, the tickets they're assigned to, and the tickets they have resolved. Users must be able to see the list of tickets they have created, as well as the tickets they have created that have been resolved. The Help Desk Manager must be able to see all tickets assigned to a specific technician, all unresolved tickets (not closed), and all tickets for a location. The Help Desk Manager and technicians should be able to see a list of all new tickets, all assigned tickets, all resolved tickets, all unresolved (not closed) tickets, and all closed tickets.

Define the Business Process

The first step in the class design process is to define the business process. This may be simply taking a written document that defines the business process already in use, or it could be working with the *process owner* (the person most responsible for the process) and others to define a new business process. This step is always the same no matter which state the existing business process is in. You should rewrite the business process in your own words and define any terms or processes that you are unsure of. The document that results will be the input for your next step in the class design process. While you are working on defining the business process, don't worry about how the application will be implemented. For example, this case study has the user providing their login and name. It is true that this information could be retrieved from somewhere else. With the .NET programming languages, it's possible to use Active Directory to retrieve information about a user, as well as the login of the currently logged in user (remember the My namespace from the previous chapter). However, at this point in the development process you should not worry about how those things are going to be implemented. You can deal with these issues when you are ready to actually implement the methods that are being defined during this step.

Case Study: Define the Business Process

First, break the business process down into steps, so that you can handle all of the peripheral actions that need to take place. For example, the business process states that technicians and the Help Desk Manager must be able to view certain information. While this not in the sequence of a process flow, it must be captured. The rewritten business process may look something like the steps listed next.

Help Desk System: Ticket Creation Process

1. The user creates a new help desk ticket providing their login name, their first name, last name, phone number, location, e-mail address, and problem description. The user chooses a category for the ticket and submits.

2. The date created and the login used must be captured.

3. The status of the ticket is new.

4. The technician views the list of new tickets.

5. The technician views the new ticket.

6. The technician sets an importance of either high, medium, or low.

7. The technician may add any additional comments.

8. The technician assigns the ticket to himself.

9. The status is changed to "assigned" and the assigned date is set.

10. The technician performs work on the ticket.

11. If the technician must wait for parts or other support, the status is set to pending.

12. The technician completes the work.

13. The technician provides a resolution and records the amount of time spent on the ticket in minutes.

14. The technician sets the status to "resolved," and records the date resolved.

15. The user is notified of the resolved ticket.

16. If the user is satisfied with the resolution, the user sets the status to closed, and the date closed is recorded.

17. If the user is not satisfied with the resolution, the user sets the status to "not resolved" and a notification is sent to the technician.

Help Desk System: Technician Views

- Technician can see a list of new tickets for their location.

- Technician can see a list of tickets assigned to them.

- Technician can see a list of tickets they resolved.

Help Desk System: User Views

- The user can see a list of tickets they've created.

- The user can see a list of tickets they've created and resolved.

Help Desk System: Help Desk Manager Views

- The Help Desk Manager can see a list of all the tickets assigned to a specific technician.

- The Help Desk Manager can see a list of all tickets for any location.

Help Desk System: Help Desk Manager and Technician Views

- The technicians and the Help Desk Manger can see a list of all new tickets.

- The technicians and the Help Desk Manager can see a list of all assigned tickets.

- The technicians and the Help Desk Manager can see a list of all resolved tickets.

- The technicians and the Help Desk Manager can see a list of all unresolved (not closed) tickets.

- The technicians and the Help Desk Manager can see a list of all closed tickets.

After listing each step of the process, it may be a good idea to create a flowchart that shows the business process flow as you understand it. The flowchart for the business process in our case study is shown in Figure 7-1.

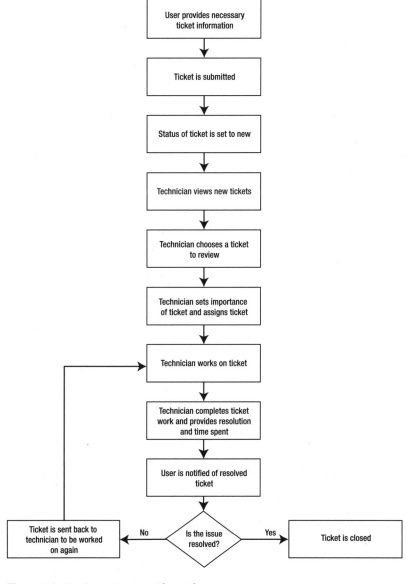

Figure 7-1. *Business Process Flow Chart*

Review the Business Process

The second step in the class design process begins with the output of the first step that we just covered—a document in your own words that defines the business process that the application is to facilitate, along with a flowchart to show the business process flow visually. This second step involves meeting with the process owner to discuss the business process and go over your initial document. There is a chance that you will have misinterpreted an item in the business process or that after reading your summation of the process, the process owner will realize that something is missing or incorrect in your understanding of the process. This could be anything from the result of a miscommunication to a process owner forgetting a step in the process. Your reviewed document will be an input for the next step in the class design process.

Break Down the Business Process

The input for this next step is the *reviewed* business process document written in your own words, along with any definitions that may be required. In this step, you'll pull out, or categorize, the nouns, adjectives, and verbs (or actions) that you'll need to complete the business process.

First, you'll begin pulling out the various nouns in the business process that may become classes. Next, you'll want to pull out all of the adjectives that relate to each noun. The adjectives may become the *properties* of a class. Then, continue your breaking down of the business process by pulling out all of the actions from the business process. These may become the methods of the class or classes.

Finally, you'll need to review the business process and your potential classes, properties, and methods, as well as determine any supporting classes, properties, or methods. These will be the most difficult to define as they are not listed specifically within the business process and must be inferred.

For example, there is required information that must be provided in order to create a new ticket. The validation that this data is in fact present can be performed in several ways. One way is to add a method called Validate ticket that includes the validation logic. The Validate ticket method would then be a supporting method for a class. The resulting document of classes, properties, and methods will be the input for the next step in the class design process. Again, at this point in the development process you don't care about how the methods that are being defined are going to be implemented. That will come in time.

Case Study: Break Down the Business Process

Begin the breakdown step by first finding the nouns that appear to represent various classes. For our case study, the result would be the classes in the following section.

Potential Classes

- Ticket

- User

- Technician

- Help Desk Manager

Next, find all of the adjectives that describe the previous nouns. These will be the potential properties. In this case the result would be:

- Ticket (noun)

  - User login name

  - First name

  - Last name

  - Phone number

  - Location

  - E-mail address

  - Problem description

  - Category

  - Date created

  - Created by login

  - Status

  - Importance

  - Additional comments

  - Assigned to

  - Resolution

  - Time spent in minutes

  - Date resolved

- Date closed

- Ticket ID

- User

- Technician

- Help Desk Manager

As you can see from this breakdown, the adjectives all describe the class called Ticket. So maybe the other classes are not necessary. This will be determined later. The next step is to define the actions for each potential class (noun). The resulting list would be:

- Ticket

  - Create new ticket

  - Assign ticket

- User

  - Ticket not resolved

  - Close ticket

  - List of tickets created

  - List of resolved tickets

- Technician

  - List of new tickets

  - List of tickets assigned to them

  - List of tickets they resolved

  - List of all new tickets

  - List of all assigned tickets

  - List of all resolved tickets

  - List of all unresolved tickets

  - List of all closed tickets

- Help Desk Manager

  - List of all tickets for a specific technician

  - List of all tickets for a specific location

  - List of all new tickets

  - List of all assigned tickets

  - List of all resolved tickets

  - List of all unresolved tickets

  - List of all closed tickets

The actions listed previously are the most obvious actions that need to take place. However, many other actions must take place that may not be so obvious. These are called *supporting actions*. The supporting actions and their potential classes are listed next:

- Ticket

  - Update ticket

  - Validate ticket

  - Change status

  - Resolve ticket

  - Notification of resolved ticket

  - Notification of not resolved ticket

- User

- Technician

- Help Desk Manager

As you can see, most of the supporting actions are dealing with the Ticket class. This is because the majority of the business process involves the ticket. It would appear that the majority of the business process really involves the technician, since the technician is performing most of the actions. However, there is a difference between the object *performing* actions and an object having actions performed *on* it.

Here's the resulting complete list of potential classes, properties, and methods that will be used as input into the next step:

- Ticket

    - Create new ticket

    - Assign ticket

    - Update ticket

    - Validate ticket

    - Change status

    - Resolve ticket

    - Notification of resolved ticket

    - Notification of not resolved ticket

- User

    - Ticket not resolved

    - Close ticket

    - List of tickets created

    - List of resolved tickets

- Technician

    - List of new tickets

    - List of tickets assigned to them

    - List of tickets they resolved

    - List of all new tickets

    - List of all assigned tickets

    - List of all resolved tickets

    - List of all unresolved tickets

    - List of all closed tickets

- Help Desk Manager

  - List of all tickets for a specific technician

  - List of all tickets for a specific location

  - List of all new tickets

  - List of all assigned tickets

  - List of all resolved tickets

  - List of all unresolved tickets

  - List of all closed tickets

Create the Class or Classes

The input for this next step is a document that groups the potential classes, properties, and methods together. From this list of potential classes, properties, and methods, you must determine which classes make the most sense. There may be multiple classes that are very similar, and it may make sense to create them as one class or as inherited from a base class. Remember from the inheritance chapter that if an "is a" relationship exists, then inheritance may be used. From your potential list of classes you must determine which classes make the most sense for this application and also determine whether additional classes must be defined. After determining your final list of classes, create a complete list of those final classes. This list of classes will be the input for the next step in the class design process.

Now that you have defined all of the potential classes, properties, and methods, you must make a determination as to the best way to group the functionality required by the application. There really is no correct set of classes, properties, and methods. No one will look at your code and say, "You must rewrite this application because you made the wrong selections." However, your decision regarding which classes, properties, and methods to use will have a large effect on the amount of work required to develop the application, not to mention the amount of effort required later for maintenance. If the class definitions are either too narrow or too broad, linking the classes together to build the required functionality may be difficult. There is nothing wrong with redefining classes later in the development process. However, be aware that the later in the development process you redefine your classes, the more impact that decision will have. Also be aware that if you change the class definition that will be used by other developers, you must notify them because they are going from the same initial specification that you started with.

In this case, most of the properties and methods are part of the ticket class. This should make sense to you, as the majority of actions and adjectives in the business process describe the ticket. Again, just because the technician performs the work and interacts with the ticket does not mean the Technician class should have the majority of the properties and methods. Think about the Ticket class as being an object in the real world. If the help desk ticket business process was purely on paper, the majority of the information would reside on a piece of paper called a ticket. The technician would then just interact with the piece of paper. The same is true in this case study—the ticket is the object with the majority of actions and attributes and the technician is simply the object that interacts with the ticket object the most.

So now take a look at your list of classes, properties, and methods. You'll notice that the technician and help desk manager are not that distinct from one another. They share a lot of the same methods or actions. Should there be two separate objects then? The answer is no.

In this case study, the technician and the help desk manager are really just security roles that have different permissions. Technicians, for example, can only see tickets for their specific location, while the help desk manager can see tickets for all locations. Both objects can see all new tickets.

The best way to approach this situation is to create a base class called Help Desk User. From that base class, inherit the core methods that both the technician and help desk manager share. The resulting derived classes should be called Technician and Help Desk Manager. The reason that inheritance (derived and base classes) can be used here is that an "is a" relationship exists. Technicians and help desk managers are both Help Desk Users. However, the Technician class will have only the methods specific to the technician role and the Help Desk Manager class will only have the methods specific to the help desk manager role. The resulting set of classes will be:

- Ticket

- User

- Help Desk User

- Technician (inherits from Help Desk User)

- Help Desk Manager (inherits from Help Desk User)

You will notice that the Technician and Help Desk Manager classes will inherit from the Help Desk User class. This list of classes will be used as input into the next step in the process—also known as defining the properties and methods of each class.

Define the Properties and Methods of Each Class

The input for this step is a document that lists the application's classes and another document that groups the potential classes, properties, and methods together. Now you'll need to map the potential properties and methods from the document listing the potential classes to the document listing the application's classes.

After mapping these properties and methods, you must determine if these properties and methods make sense for the various classes. If they do, then add them to the class. If they don't, then you must determine if another class is required or if the properties or methods can be placed within another class. You shouldn't just drop a property or method that doesn't appear to fit into any of the classes unless you very sure that property or method is not necessary. The next step is to determine if there are additional properties or methods that must be included with each class for the application. If there are, add these to the appropriate class. The list of classes, their properties, and methods will be the input for the next step in the class design process.

Case Study: Define the Properties and Methods of Each Class

Now that you have defined your classes, you must formally determine the properties and methods. To begin, bring forward the list of potential classes, properties, and methods from your earlier list. The list of potential classes and methods was:

- Ticket

  - Create new ticket

  - Assign ticket

  - Update ticket

  - Validate ticket

  - Change status

  - Resolve ticket

  - Notification of resolved ticket

  - Notification of not resolved ticket

- User

  - Ticket not resolved

  - Close ticket

  - List of tickets created

  - List of resolved tickets

- Technician

    - List of new tickets

    - List of tickets assigned to them

    - List of tickets they resolved

    - List of all new tickets

    - List of all assigned tickets

    - List of all resolved tickets

    - List of all unresolved tickets

    - List of all closed tickets

- Help Desk Manager

    - List of all tickets for a specific technician

    - List of all tickets for a specific location

    - List of all new tickets

    - List of all assigned tickets

    - List of all resolved tickets

    - List of all unresolved tickets

    - List of all closed tickets

The potential list of classes and properties was:

- Ticket

    - User login name

    - First name

    - Last name

    - Phone number

    - Location

- E-mail address

- Problem description

- Category

- Date created

- Created by login

- Status

- Importance

- Additional comments

- Assigned to

- Resolution

- Time spent in minutes

- Date resolved

- Date closed

- Ticket ID

- User

- Technician

- Help Desk Manager

Now map the original potential classes, properties, and methods to the classes that were determined to be the best:

- Ticket

  - User login name

  - First name

  - Last name

  - Phone number

  - Location

- E-mail address

- Problem description

- Category

- Date created

- Created by login

- Status

- Importance

- Additional comments

- Assigned to

- Resolution

- Time spent in minutes

- Date resolved

- Date closed

- Ticket ID

- Create new ticket

- Assign ticket

- Update ticket

- Validate ticket

- Change status

- Resolve ticket

- Notification of resolved ticket

- Notification of not resolved ticket

- User

  - Ticket not resolved

  - Close ticket

- List of tickets created

- List of resolved tickets

- Is Technician

- Is Help Desk Manager

- Help Desk User

  - List of new tickets

  - List of all assigned tickets

  - List of all resolved tickets

  - List of all unresolved tickets

  - List of all closed tickets

- Technician (inherits from Help Desk User)

  - List of tickets assigned to them

  - List of tickets they resolved

- Help Desk Manager (inherits from Help Desk User)

  - List of all tickets for a specific technician

  - List of all tickets for a specific location

Notice that this is a complete list of properties and methods for each class. Also notice that two new properties have been added to the user class. The Is Technician user class property will be used to determine whether the user is a technician or a general user. The Is Help Desk Manager user class property will be used to determine if the user is a help desk manager. This completed list is now the input for the next and final step in the class design process, creating the classes in VB.NET.

Create the Class Structure

This is the final step in the class design process and it takes the list of classes, their properties, and their methods as its input. From the list of classes, you'll need to create a new class file for each class listed. Within each class defined within the list, you'll need to define a local private variable for each property. For each property that needs to be public, you'll need to create a public property structure. For each property that needs to be private, you do not create a property structure, but can just leave the variable defined as private. For each method, determine whether it should be public or private and then define it as such. Next, determine if each method requires a parameter or not—if so, define that parameter. Finally, for each method, determine whether the method should return a value If the method should *not* return a value, then define the method as a sub. The output of this last step will be the output of the class design process, also known as the completed class structure.

Now is also a good time to look for reusable classes. If your company has a class library or namespace that contains common functionality, now is the time to determine if any preexisting functionality can be used in your application. It's possible that a class may already exist for getting user information, for example. You will need to compare the methods and properties that you need to the methods and properties that exist for the common class. If your class needs the common functionality along with additional functionality, then you will want to inherit the common class and then add your own functionality. That added functionality may come in the form of new methods or properties or by an overriding of existing methods.

Case Study: Create the Class Structure

To begin this part of the class design process, create a new web site called HelpDesk. After creating the new web site, create a new class file for each class. To do so, right-click on the web site URL in the Solution Explorer and choose Add New Item.

When the Add New Item window appears, choose Class. Provide the class name as shown in the design, but without the spaces.

After clicking Add for each class, you will receive a message similar to the one shown in Figure 7-2. Click Yes. This message tells you that the class file (.vb file) you are creating will be created within the App_Code folder within the web site.

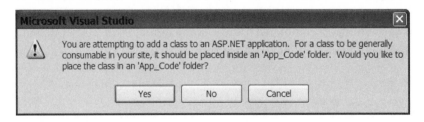

Figure 7-2. *A check for where to put the class page*

After adding all of the classes, your Solution Explorer should look like Figure 7-3.

Now that the classes have been designed and the .vb files have been created, it's time to determine how each method of each class will be implemented. For example, this is a good time to determine how to get the user's information, such as name and e-mail address. There are several ways you can get this information based on your environment. You might look this information up in a database or directory services such as Active Directory, for

Figure 7-3. *Solution Explorer with classes listed*

example. Either way, now is the time for you to determine how to implement each method.

Since the Help Desk User class is a base class, it should be created first. It must be created *before* the other two can be created, so that they can inherit from the base class. To begin, open the HelpDeskUser.vb file.

There are several methods that you'll need to create for the Help Desk User class. I will define these next. However, I won't enter any code for them since they require a connection to a database. Instead, each method will return a Dataset, which is used to store data:

```
Public Function RetrieveNewTickets() As Data.DataSet

End Function
Public Function RetrieveAllAssignedTickets() As Data.DataSet

End Function
Public Function RetrieveAllResolvedTickets() As Data.DataSet

End Function
Public Function RetrieveAllUnresolvedTickets() As Data.DataSet

End Function
Public Function RetrieveAllClosedTickets() As Data.DataSet

End Function
```

After creating the Help Desk User class, you need to create the Technician and Help Desk Manager classes. As mentioned previously, they need to be created after the Help Desk User class since they inherit from it. To begin, open the Technician class page. Just under the opening class line (Public Class Technician), add Inherits helpdeskuser, as shown in Figure 7-4.

```
Imports Microsoft.VisualBasic

Public Class Technician
    Inherits he
    Private
                  Group
                  GroupCollection
    Public        Handlers
                  Hashtable
    End Fur       HelpDeskManager
    Public        HelpDeskUser
                  HiddenField
    End Fur       HiddenFieldPageStatePersister
                  HierarchicalDataBoundControl
    Public        HierarchicalDataSourceControl
        str
                  Common                    All
```

Figure 7-4. *Inheriting from HelpDeskUser*

After you set the inherits, you need to add the remaining methods. The Technician class design looked like:

- Technician (inherits from Help Desk User)

  - List of tickets assigned to them

  - List of tickets they resolved

Declare a private variable called strUserName, which is a string. This will hold the login name of the user for use within this class. Now you need to build a constructor to assign the login. You'll remember that a constructor is a sub that always has the name New and must always be a sub. A constructor is the first method called when the class is initiated. This is done automatically when you declare a variable with the New keyword, such as clsTicket = New Ticket. The purpose of the constructor is to allow you to perform some actions when the class is created. Often, constructors are used to set variables that will be used throughout the class or to set or reset values. You can have multiple constructors by defining multiple subs called New, each with a different parameter set. For this class, there will be one parameter called UserLogin that will be a string.

To create the New sub, select Technician from the top left drop-down list, if it is not already selected. Next, choose New from the top right drop-down list. This will automatically create the New sub structure. After the New sub structure is in place, add a parameter called UserName that is defined as a string. Assign the value from the UserLogin parameter to the local variable strUserName as shown here:

```
Public Sub New(ByVal UserLogin As String)
strUserName = UserLogin
End Sub
```

Next declare the two methods as functions that return a Data.Dataset data type:

```
Public Function AssignedToMe() As Data.DataSet

End Function
Public Function ResolvedByMe() As Data.DataSet

End Function
```

Next, open the HelpDeskManager.vb file. Add the `Inherits HelpDeskUser` line of code again, just like with the Technician class. The Help Desk Manager class design looked like:

- Help Desk Manager (inherits from Help Desk User)

    - List of all tickets for a specific technician

    - List of all tickets for a specific location

Create and code a New sub with a parameter of UserLogin, the same way you did for the Technician class. Next, declare the two methods as functions that return a Data.Dataset data type. The first method will be RetrieveTicketsForLocation, with a parameter of Location, which will be a string data type. The second method will be RetrieveTicketsForTechnician, with a parameter of Technician, which will be a string data type:

```
Public Function RetrieveTicketsForLocation(ByVal Location As String)
As Data.DataSet

End Function
Public Function RetrieveTicketsForTechnician(ByVal Technician As String)
As Data.DataSet

End Function
```

Now that the base and derived classes are completed, open the User.vb file. The user class design was:

- User

    - Ticket not resolved

    - Close ticket

    - List of tickets created

    - List of resolved tickets

- Is Technician

- Is Help Desk Manager

The user class has two properties: Is Technician and Is Help Desk Manager. Both will be defined as Boolean and will be read-only. The reason these properties will be read-only is that when the class is created, a determination will be made based on the user's login as to whether the user is a technician or a help desk manager. To set this class up, declare a private variable called blnIsTechnician that is defined as a Boolean, and declare a private variable called blnIsHelpDeskManager that is defined as a Boolean. After defining the two variables, create a public read-only property for each variable called IsTechnician and IsHelpDeskManager, respectively. The code for these two public properties will look like this:

```
Private blnIsTechnician As Boolean
Private blnIsHelpDeskManager As Boolean

Public ReadOnly Property IsTechnician() As Boolean
Get
Return blnIsTechnician
End Get
End Property

Public ReadOnly Property IsHelpDeskManager() As Boolean
Get
Return blnIsHelpDeskManager
End Get
End Property
```

Next, you need to build a constructor to determine whether the user is a technician or help desk manager. For this class, there will be one parameter called UserLogin that will be a string. To create the New sub, select User from the top left drop-down list, if it is not already selected. Next choose New from the top right drop-down list. This will automatically create the New sub structure. After the New sub structure is in place, add a parameter called UserLogin that is defined as a string. Typically in this sub, you would want to write code that will determine whether the user is a technician or help desk manager. This would probably best include code to retrieve security information from a database.

Again, since the database interaction is outside the scope of this book, just type `blnIsTechnician = True` and `blnIsHelpDeskManager=False`. This will set the local variable blnIsTechnician to true and will set the local variable blnIsHelpDeskManager to false, which results in:

```
Public Sub New(ByVal UserLogin As String)
blnIsTechnician = True
blnIsHelpDeskManager = False
End Sub
```

Next create the methods for this class. The first method will require a parameter that is the ticket id of the ticket to set as "not resolved." The first method doesn't require a return value. The second method will require a parameter that is the ticket id of the ticket to be set as "closed." The second method doesn't require a return value either. The third and fourth methods will require a UserName parameter that is a string used to provide the name of the user you want to retrieve records for. Again, the most efficient way to return the list is to return a Data.DataSet. Therefore, methods three and four will have a return type of Data.DataSet. The user class code will look like:

```
Public Sub TicketNotResolved(ByVal TicketID As Integer)

End Sub
Public Sub CloseTicket(ByVal TicketID As Integer)

End Sub
Public Function TicketsCreatedByMe(ByVal UserName As String) As Data.DataSet

End Function
Public Function MyResolvedTickets(ByVal UserName As String) As Data.DataSet

End Function
```

Finally, the last class to be built will be the Ticket class. This class will require the most amount of code.

Each of the properties needs to have both a private and public variable defined for it. To begin, open the Ticket class file. Within the Ticket class structure, add a private variable for the user login. This should be a string value. The declaration should be `Private strUserLogin as string`.

After declaring the private variable, you should also create a public property by typing `Public Property UserLoginName as string` and pressing Enter. When you press Enter, the public property structure will appear.

Within the lines `Get` and `End Get`, type `Return strUserLogin`. Between the lines `Set` and `End Set`, type `strUserLogin = value`.

Continue this pattern for all of the properties. The private variable declarations will look like this:

```
Private strUserLogin As String
Private strFirstName As String
Private strLastName As String
Private strPhoneNumber As String
Private intLocation As Integer
Private strEmailAddress As String
Private strProblemDescription As String
Private strCategory As String
Private strCreatedByLogin As String
Private strStatus As String
Private strImportance As String
Private strAdditionalComments As String
Private strAssignedTo As String
Private strResolution As String
Private decTimeSpent As Decimal
Private dteDateResolved As Date
Private intTicketID as Integer
Private dteDateClosed As Date
```

After adding all of the public properties, look at the methods. The class design for the methods is:

- Create new ticket

- Assign ticket

- Update ticket

- Validate ticket

- Change status

- Resolve ticket

- Notification of resolved ticket

- Notification of not resolved ticket

The first method will not require a parameter because it will create the ticket. It's a good idea to return a Boolean when creating or updating a ticket, so that the calling application knows that the code has completed successfully. The Assign Ticket and Update Ticket methods will require a parameter for the ticket id and return a Boolean value denoting that they have completed. The Validate Ticket method is a private function to determine whether the data entered is valid. The Change Status method will require a parameter for the ticket id and a parameter for the status id. It should also include a return Boolean value. The Resolve Ticket method will require a parameter for the ticket id and a return Boolean value. The Notification of Resolved Ticket method and the Notification of Not Resolved method will require a parameter for the ticket id, an e-mail address parameter, and a returned Boolean. The completed method declarations will look like:

```
Public Function NewTicket() As Boolean

End Function
Public Function AssignTicket(ByVal TicketID As Integer) As Boolean

End Function
Public Function UpdateTicket(ByVal TicketID As Integer) As Boolean

End Function
Private Function ValidateTicket() As Boolean

End Function
Public Function ChangeStatus(ByVal TicketID As Integer,
ByVal StatusID As Integer) As Boolean

End Function
Public Function ResolveTicket(ByVal TicketID As Integer) As Boolean

End Function
Public Function NotificationOfResolved(ByVal TicketID As Integer,
ByVal EmailAddress As String) As Boolean

End Function
    Public Function NotificationOfNotResolved(ByVal TicketID As Integer,
ByVal EmailAddress As String) As Boolean

End Function
```

After you create all of the public properties and the methods you need, you might notice that the code page gets a little difficult to navigate. You can use a special tag within VS2005, known as # Region, to create a code region.

For example, prior to the first Public Property statement, you might enter #Region "Public Properties". (Make *sure* you have the quotes around the name of the region.) After the last End Property enter #End Region. This will create a code region. Now go back to the beginning of the code region, and you should see a minus sign next to the #Region tag. Clicking that minus sign will collapse the region, so that you will only see the name of the region, rather than all of the public property code. This is a nice way to organize your code.

Now that you've built the skeleton for all of your classes, you can concentrate on implementing each method. Again, since ADO.NET is outside the scope of this book, many of the methods can't be implemented. However, other methods can be implemented to a point.

The first method to implement is the AddTicket method. There are several ways to validate input into a class and subsequently into a database. For one, you can define constraints within the database that will validate the data when it is being entered into the database. The problem with this strategy is that the error messages returned from SQL Server are not very user-friendly and will need to be interpreted before they are shown to the user.

Another way to provide validation is to add a private method (like ValidateTicket), which will verify all necessary data that has been provided to the public properties before an attempt is made to push the data to the database.

The third way to validate data is at the user interface level, by using the validator control that is discussed in Chapter 9. My personal preference is to combine the last two options. This way you can create a validation method to make sure the values have been passed to the necessary properties and also use the validator control to show the user the data that fails validation. Therefore, the first method that needs to be implemented, even before the AddTicket method, is the ValidateTicket method.

Within the structure of the ValidateTicket method, add code to make sure that the user login, first name, last name, e-mail address, location, category, and problem description public properties all have values. First, there must be some way to collect the list of invalid properties to be returned. So, create a local string variable within the ValidateTicket method called strErrors. The code should look like this:

```
If strUserLogin.Length = 0 Then
strErrors = strErrors & "User Login not provided,"
End If
```

Continue that pattern for each of the public properties mentioned for testing. After you add all of the code needed to validate the public properties, you need to have a way to let the calling method know there was a problem. This is done by determining whether strErrors contains a string (has error messages) and if it does, throwing it an exception:

```
If strErrors.length > 0  Then
strErrors = Mid(strErrors, 1, strErrors.length - 1)
Throw New Exception("Errors have occured: " & strErrors)
Else
Return True
End If
```

This first line determines whether the length of strErrors is greater than zero. If there were errors, then the length of strErrors would be greater than zero and the next line would be executed.

The second line removes the last comma from the value of strErrors by reassigning the value of strErrors from the first character to the character that is one less than the length (also known as the second to last character). This will produce a string that has the last character stripped from it. The third line will throw an exception object and give it a message to pass along. The Else part of the statement will return true if strErrors has no characters in it.

The ValidateTicket function needs to be called from the NewTicket method within a Try . . . Catch block in order to be used. The Try . . . Catch block is the way that VB.NET and C# handle exceptions. The first line is always Try followed by the lines of code that could cause an exception. After the code that might cause an exception, the Catch block is added. The Catch block can be used to catch a variety of exceptions. The Catch block is also used to determine what to do when an exception is encountered. In this case, the keyword Throw will be used to raise the exception to the code that invoked the current code. You should have Try . . . Catch blocks within each layer of code, and with each block within the user interface displaying the exception. I'll discuss the concept of displaying the exception in Chapter 8. For now, add the following code to the AddTicket method:

```
Try
If ValidateTicket() Then
intTicketID = 10
return True
End If
Catch ex As Exception
Throw New Exception(ex.ToString)
End Try
```

As you can see, the first line starts the Try . . . Catch block. The second line calls the ValidateTicket private method in order to determine whether the public properties were provided. Since this sample application will not be tied to a database, I assigned 10 to the private variable intTicketID. This is the line used to take the database-generated ID and give it back to the calling code. If everything is all right with the validation, then True can be returned—otherwise an exception will be thrown. If any of the public properties are not provided, an exception will be thrown from the ValidateTicket method and will also be caught within the Catch block. Within the Catch block, the Throw line lets the .NET Framework know what to do with any exception that the block catches. In this case, the action is to throw the exception again, but to a higher level where it can be better dealt with. You will see in Chapter 8 that the higher level (the user interface) will catch the exception and display it.

Other methods within this class might also require some validation, but will probably not need the use of an entire method for their testing. For example, the AssignTicket method will first validate that the AssignedTo public property has been provided. If the user that the ticket is assigned to is not provided, then the ticket can't be assigned. To accomplish this, use another Try . . . Catch block that throws a new exception if the AssignedTo public property has not been provided. The code will look like this:

```
Try
If strAssignedTo.length=0 Then
Throw New Exception("Assigned To not provided")
End If
Catch ex As Exception
Throw New Exception(ex.ToString)
End Try
```

Conclusion

In this chapter, I've defined a process for designing classes as well as provided you with a step-by-step approach to the process. You also learned, in this chapter, to create a web site for a help desk application with several classes. You found that all of the classes have methods, and that some of them have the beginnings of implementation in them.

In the next chapter I'll show you how to create web forms that can be used within the web site that use the classes you've created here. As I've mentioned, there won't be very much functionality built into these classes yet, as ADO.NET is outside the scope of this book. However, you *will* learn how to code the user interface to make calls to the AddTicket and AssignTo methods as well as learning how to assign the public properties to the Ticket class. You will also learn how to step through the code to get a glimpse of how the exception handling is done.

■ ■ ■

CHAPTER 8

ASP.NET Web Forms

In this chapter, I'll provide an introduction to ASP.NET web forms by first providing an overview of how web forms work and then showing you how to use them to develop a web site. I'll expand on the previous chapter by adding forms to the web site that you created in Chapter 7. The forms will help to create more of a functioning site.

Using the Web Forms Designer

Before you can add a web form to your web site, you need to understand how both the Web Forms Designer and the Page class works. The Web Forms Designer is the tool within VS2005 that allows you to design and build web forms. To begin designing and building your web forms with Web Forms Designer, create a new web site project called Chapter8. When the web site project is created the area in the center of the screen that you see is the Web Forms Designer.

Notice that there are several tabs at the bottom of the Web Forms Designer window. The tab that is highlighted by default is labeled Design. The Design tab of the Web Forms Designer allows you to design the form by adding controls from the toolbox. The Source tab displays the HTML source code that will be used by web browsers to display the web form. You must have clicked on the Source view to see the HTML source. While in the Source view, you can click on the other tabs at the bottom to the right of the Source tab. These tabs include HTML and Body by default. When you click one of these tabs the HTML source within those HTML tags is highlighted.

Note HTML tags are out of the scope of this book. However, you should be familiar with HTML tags when creating web forms, although it is not required. HTML tags are simply used to define the web form in a way that Internet browsers can understand. The Web Forms Designer automatically creates the HTML tags that are needed for a web form that is defined within VS2005.

For example, if you click the Body tag, all HTML tags between the opening Body tag and the closing Body tag are highlighted, as shown in Figure 8-1. This allows you to verify both the opening and closing tags are there and helps with tag organization.

```
<html xmlns="http://www.w3.org/1999/xhtml" >
<head runat="server">
    <title>Untitled Page</title>
</head>
<body>
    <form id="form1" runat="server">
    <div>

    </div>
    </form>
</body>
</html>
```

Figure 8-1. *Content of Body tags*

Adding Controls

The Web Forms Designer allows you to design forms without creating the HTML that is required for the Internet browsers to display the page. Instead, you can drag and drop web form controls from the Toolbox onto your page. After you drop the control on the form you can move it around and resize it, as well as provide values for various properties.

The Toolbox appears on the left side of the Web Forms Designer by default and is shown in Figure 8-2.

Figure 8-2. *Web Forms Designer Toolbox*

The ASP.NET Page Class

A web form created by the Web Forms Designer, along with any code that is associated with that particular page, makes up an ASP.NET page. When a page is compiled, a new class derived (inherited from) the base Page class is generated and compiled. The base class is System.Web.UI.Page. If the page contains controls, the Page class is a container for the controls. An instance of each control is created at run time and then that control renders output that the browser can understand. Since the ASP.NET page is a class, it has properties, methods, and events similar to any other class. The ASP.NET Page class raises events, and you can write event handlers that execute when an event is raised. To view the possible events for the page, open the Default.aspx.vb code file.

After the code page appears, click the drop down list at the top left of the Designer that says General. Select Page Events from the list, as shown in Figure 8-3.

Figure 8-3. *Choosing Page Events*

After choosing the Page Events category from the left drop-down list, go to the drop-down list on the right to see all of the page events as shown in Figure 8-4.

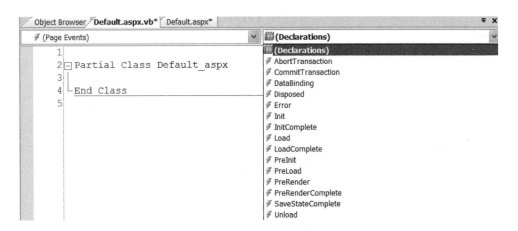

Figure 8-4. *List of Page Events*

To write code that will be executed when one of the events occurs, click the page event on the right drop-down list that you want to trigger your code. For example, to add code to the Load event, choose Load, as shown in Figure 8-5.

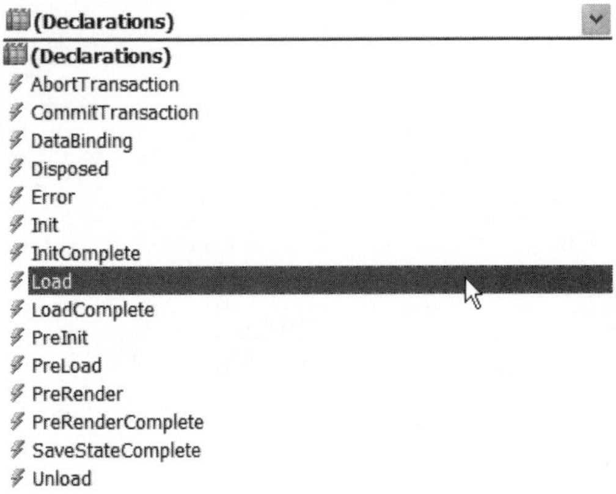

Figure 8-5. *Choosing the Load Page Event*

After choosing Load from the drop-down list the sub definition will appear. You can add your code here to be executed when the load event is triggered.

Page Lifecycle

All web forms have a *life cycle*, which is the process that each form goes through. Understanding this process or life cycle will help you understand where to place your code and when that code will be executed.

Round Trips

It is also very helpful to remember that all web pages by nature are *stateless*. Stateless means that they are not connected to the web server at all times. When an HTML page is called from a browser client, the web server sends the HTML content to the browser. Then, the browser interprets the HTML content and displays it. Once the HTML is received by the browser, the connection to the server is disconnected. This process of sending HTML content to the client browser and then the client browser responding back to the server is called a *round trip*. In web forms, most of the user actions result in a round trip. For example, the click of a button on a web form by the user generates a round trip to the server to determine what to do when that button is clicked. Since each time an event is triggered a round trip is made, most controls do not have an event for mouse over. This would require too many round trips.

View State

View state is a server control property that allows the saving and restoration of information in the control across multiple requests to the same page. The view state property is enabled for all server controls by default. When a page is processed, the current state of the page and its controls are combined into a string and then saved in the page as a hidden field. When the page is sent back to the server, the page parses this string and restores the property information to the page. Since this is done automatically, you don't need to be concerned with losing data from one user action to the next. For example, if a user clicks a Save button, but you have a validation routine that determines the information can't be saved, there is no need to determine the values that were in any of the controls on the form when the user clicked the Save button. Those values will appear in the controls, so the user can view them again if necessary.

To see this working, open the Help Desk web site (if it's not already open). Then, open the Default.aspx page. Place a text box control and a button on the form. Start the application by choosing Start without debugging from the Debug menu. This action will just start the application and will not attempt to debug it. When you see that the Default.aspx page is displayed, type **text** into the text box and click the button. Notice the data is still there. If you right-click within the browser window and choose View Source, the HTML source code will appear. You'll notice an input tag of type hidden with a name __VIEWSTATE. This is a hidden text box that contains a hash of the contents of the form. This text box stores the information that is kept between page uses. (In previous versions of ASP the developer needed to move those values forward from one page to the next.)

Web Form Processing Stages

Here's an outline of the most common processing scenario:

- ASP.NET Page Framework initialized

    - The Page Init event is executed.

    - The page and control view state are restored.

- User code initialized

    - The Page Load event is executed.

    - Stored values are read and restored.

- Validation

- The Validate method of any validator control is executed.

- Event Handling

  - Any events triggered by the user are handled and their actions taken.

- Clean Up

  - The Unload event is executed.

  - Close any database connections and discard objects no longer needed.

One interesting detail about the Page Load event is you can use the IsPostBack property of the Page class to determine whether the page is being loaded at the request of a control on the form or the page is being loaded for the first time. Each control also has an AutoPostBack property. By default, buttons are set to true and all other controls are set to false. But when a control with an Autopostback property (which is false by default) has a value of true and is interacted with (either by clicking a button or selecting an item from a drop-down list) the page is requested again and the IsPostBack property of the page is true. This is best used if you have actions such as retrieving default data or setting control properties that you want to have happen the first time the page is displayed but not when the page is loaded at any time afterwards. To use IsPostBack, the following lines of code can be placed within the Page Load event handler:

```
If Not IsPostBack then
'Retrieve initial data to display
End If
```

You can also add an Else clause to perform some work if the page has been requested by a control (posted back).

Session and Application Objects

ASP.NET maintains information about various processes while a web site is running. These include the current application and each user session. The information about user sessions maintained by ASP.NET and the application is stored in classes. The HTTPApplicationState class provides application-wide methods and events for all sessions as well as access to the application-wide cache that stores information. The HTTPSessionState object provides information to the current user session and provides a session-wide cache you can use to store information in.

Application Object

An instance of the HTTPApplicationState class is created the first time any client requests a page within the virtual directory of an ASP.NET application. The HTTPApplicationState is very similar to a global variable from VB6. The value is held across the entire application, no matter where it was assigned. The value can also be changed from anywhere within the application. The HTTPApplicationState class allows you to add key value pairs that store and retrieve information about the application. You can use this to store and retrieve information that is specific to the entire application, such as a connection string to a certain database. If you do choose to use the application object, be very careful. Remember, the application object holds information that can be changed from anywhere within the application. So you might have code on one page that changes the value and then you might call another page that changes the value as well. If you were looking for the first value you would not get it, you would get the second value. So, if you want to use the application object, use it for information that won't change. For example, you can use the application object to hold the company name to assign to the text property on a label. In the last section of this chapter, which will expand on the existing Help Desk web site, I'll show you how to set an application object to the company name and how to use that application object to retrieve the company name. You can use the intrinsic Application object to access the methods and properties of the HttpApplicationState class.

Session Object

The Session object can be accessed by just typing **Session**. You can use the Session object to store information about the specific user session. Each time a user accesses an ASP.NET site, a session is started. The session remains active until the user closes the browser. Each session is identified and tracked by ASP.NET by a session id string. The session id string can then be used to communicate across client-server requests either by using an HTTP cookie or a modified URL. The session id is generated by an algorithm and makes it difficult for a malicious user to get a new session id and determine an existing session id from that new session id. To use the session object you can use the contents collection to add the new items that you want to store information about. To do so just use the syntax:

```
Session.Contents("UserLogin") = "bmyers"
```

To retrieve the value, you can set a variable equal to the item in session.contents, such as:

```
StrLogin = Session.Contents("UserLogin").ToString
```

The ToString method needs to be used in this instance, because otherwise a warning will appear that an implicit conversion from System.Object to String is being performed. You do not need to use the ToString method, as the lack of it will not generate a compiler error, but it's best to perform this conversion. This warning occurs because Session.Contents is an object and you are attempting to assign the value of that object to a string.

Cookies

A cookie is data stored either in a text file on the client's file system or in memory in the browser. It contains a small amount of page-specific information that the server sends to the client along with page output. Cookies can be either temporary (set to expire) or persistent. Use cookies to store information about a client, session, or application. Most of the time, cookies are used to store the user names (and potentially the password of the user on the client) or to store the last page visited by the user in order to jump back into a large application. However, you should not store the password for a user within a cookie on the client computer. It's not a problem to store user names, or preferably an ID, for the user in the cookie, but it's bad practice to store the password. The reason is that the cookie is in plain text and can easily be found by a hacker who has control of a client computer.

A *good* use of a cookie is to record when the user was last on the site. Use the following code to create a new cookie that stores the last visit date:

```
Dim MyCookie As New HttpCookie("LastVisit")
Dim now As DateTime = DateTime.Now
MyCookie.Value = now.ToString()
MyCookie.Expires = now.AddHours(1)
Response.Cookies.Add(MyCookie)
```

To retrieve the contents of cookies that are stored on the client:

```
Dim MyCookieColl As HttpCookieCollection
Dim MyCookie As HttpCookie
Dim LastVisit as Date
MyCookieColl = Request.Cookies
MyCookie = MyCookieColl("LastVisit")
LastVisit = MyCookie("LastVisit").ToString
```

Expanding the Help Desk Application

Now I'll expand on the Help Desk web site that you created in Chapter 7. In that chapter you created the web site, the classes for the web site, and then you implemented some of the methods. This section will also add some of the implementation details for the business process defined in Chapter 7. This will include determining whether the currently logged-in user is a technician, help desk manager, or general user. Based on that determination, a page will be displayed for either the user console or the technician console. Next, some code will be used to either display a button if the user is a help desk manager or not display it if the user is just a help desk employee. Finally, I'll show you how to add text boxes to a form in order to gather information for a ticket, pass the values to the tickets class, and validate the information.

The first task you need to accomplish is to set the company name when the application starts and then use the application object to retrieve the company name on each page. The first step in this task is to create a global.asax file. This page will be executed the first time the application is executed and can be used to set application level variables when the application starts. To add the global.asax page, right-click the web site URL within the Solution Explorer and choose Add Item. When the Add Item window appears, choose Global Application Class. The name will default to Global.asax; leave this as the name. Click Add to add the file to the web site.

Note Once you add a Global Application Class file to a web site it won't be available to add again. A web site can only have one Global Application Class file.

When the Global.asax page has been added to the application, open the file (if it isn't already opened). You will notice an Application_Start sub. This sub will be executed each time the application is started. Notice there are also other subs such as Application_End and Application_Error. The Application_End sub will be executed when the application is shut down. You could use this to send e-mails or write to the event log if the application stops. The Application_Error sub will be executed when an error occurs anywhere within the application and is unhandled. You will also see Session subs that occur when a user session is started and ended.

Within the Application_Start sub add the following line of code:

```
Application.contents("CompanyName")="My Company Name"
```

This line of code will add a key value pair to an instance of the HTTPApplicationState class. The key is CompanyName and the value is "My Company Name". When the application is started, this line of code will be executed and the instance of the HTTPApplicationState class represented by the Application object will have this key value pair available to it.

The next step in this task is to add two "console" pages. These pages will give users a way to see a list of help desk tickets. The first console is the Technician Console. Add a new web form to the web site called TechConsole. Drag a label onto the TechConsole form and change the ID to lblPageName and set the text property to "Technician Console". The second console is the User Console. Add a new web form to the web site called UserConsole. Drag a label onto the UserConsole form, change the ID to lblPageName and then set the text property to User Console. Now there are a total of three forms within the web site (Default, TechConsole, and UserConsole). On both pages, drag a label to the form, set the ID property to lblCompanyName and then remove any value within the Text property. On each form, place this new label above the lblPageName label that you added previously.

■Tip You can add the label lblCompanyName to just one of the forms and copy and paste the label to the other form. The label will retain the ID and text properties when pasted on the second form.

The Technician Console page should look like Figure 8-6.

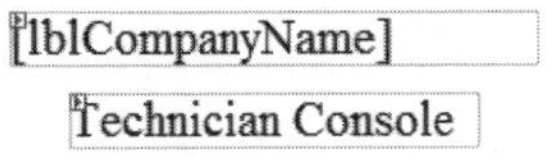

[lblCompanyName]

Technician Console

Figure 8-6. *Technician Console*

■Note Notice the lblCompanyName that appears within the lblCompanyName label. When the text property of a label is blank, the ID property of the label appears within the label so you know which label it is.

View the code for the TechConsole page. Choose Page Events from the left drop-down list at the top of the page and then choose Load from the right drop-down list at the top of the page. This will create the Page_Load sub. Within the Page_Load sub, add

```
lblCompanyName.Text = Application("CompanyName").ToString
```

This line of code will use the Application instance of the HTTPApplicationState class to find the key value CompanyName and return the value portion of the key value pair to the text property of the lblCompanyName control. This is a way of getting the value using a short notation, but you could also have used the Item property:

```
lblCompanyName.Text = Application.Item("CompanyName").ToString
```

Also, you don't need to use the name of the key—you can use the index, such as 1. However, this isn't recommended as you might change the order of the items within the Application_Start sub and cause an issue with the numbering. So it's always best to use the name of the key.

Now, copy the line of code that you just entered. Open the UserConsole page, create the Page_Load sub, and then paste the code within the Page_Load sub.

Now it is time to test the results of this task. Both the TechConsole and the UserConsole pages should have the name of the company and the name of the page at the top. Click on the TechConsole.aspx page within the Solution Explorer and then start the application without debugging. The TechConsole.aspx page should now appear. The company name should be displayed along with Technician Console, as shown in Figure 8-7.

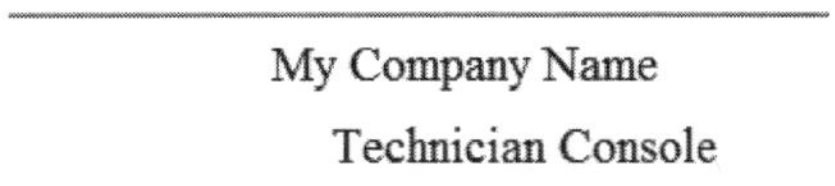

The next task is to gather the user name and determine whether that user is a technician, help desk manager, or general user. To accomplish this, a session variable will be created to hold the user's login name. Also, the Default.aspx page will be set as the default page for the web site and will determine the user's type. If the user is a technician or help desk manager they will be redirected from the

---

My Company Name

Technician Console

Figure 8-7. *Testing the Technician Console*

Default.aspx page to the Technician Console (TechConsole) page. If the user is a general user they will be redirected from the Default.aspx page to the User Console (UserConsole) page.

The first step for this task is to get the user's login name when the session starts (or when the user accesses the web site). To do this, open the Global.asax page again and find the Session_Start sub. This sub will be executed when the user accesses the web site. Each user who logs in will get their own session. To access the user's login, the virtual directory within IIS must be setup for Integrated Windows Authentication only. (This was covered in Chapter 6.) Add the following code to the Session_Start sub:

```
Dim intBegin As Integer
Dim strName As String
intBegin = InStr(My.User.Name, "\")
If intBegin > 0 Then
strName = Mid(My.User.Name, intBegin + 1, Len(My.User.Name) - intBegin)
Else
strName = My.User.Name
End If
Session.Add("UserLogin", strName)
```

Let's go through this code line by line. The first two lines of code declare variables that are to be used just within this sub. The remainder of the code tries to determine if the user name has a slash in it. The importance of this is that the name property of the User class within the My namespace will provide the windows login which includes the domain. In most cases, you do not need the domain's name, just the user's login as you are only working with one domain. (This example assumes you are only working with one domain.) Line 3 determines if there is a \ in the user name. Remember, you can get the currently logged in user's login name by using the User class within the My namespace. intBegin in line 3 will have a value of 0 if there isn't a slash in the name. Line 4 determines if there was a slash by determining if intBegin is greater than 0.

Line 5 is a little tricky. This line uses the built-in Mid function to get part of the Name property after the domain's name and the slash. The first parameter to the Mid function is the string to break apart, in this case My.User.Name. The second parameter to the Mid function is where to begin, so in this case you need to add one to intBegin. Remember intBegin will be the position of the slash within the My.User.Name string. The last parameter to the Mid function is how many characters to advance.

Use the Len function to make sure all characters are accounted for. The Len built-in function returns the length of the parameter passed to it, in this case My.User.Name. After Len returns its value, the value of intBegin is subtracted. For example, if the length of a string was 10 and intBegin was 2 the value passed as the final parameter to the Mid function would be 8. This will allow Mid to start at the position represented by intBegin and get the remaining characters of the first parameter. In the end, this will just provide the user's login name, which follows the domain's name and the slash.

Line 7 will just assign the value from the Name property of the User class of the My namespace instead of removing the domain's name.

Finally, Line 9 will add a key value pair to the Session object with a key of UserLogin. This key can be used later to get the currently logged in user.

The next step is to verify that this is working correctly. To do this, add a text box to the Default.aspx page with an ID property of txtUserName. View the code for Default.aspx or open the Default.aspx.vb file. Create the Page_Load sub by using the drop-down lists at the top of the code page. Add

```
txtUserName.Text = Session("UserLogin").ToString
```

to the Page_Load sub.

This code will find the UserLogin key within the Session object and provide the value from that key value pair to the text property of the txtUserName control. This will verify that only the user's login name is being stored in the session variable, rather than the whole user name and the domain name. Start without debugging to verify that the steps of the task were completed correctly.

After verifying that the user's login is the only part being retrieved and stored in the session object, delete the text box control and any other controls you may have placed on the Default.aspx page. View the code for the Default.aspx page or open the Default.aspx.vb file and then delete the code within the Page_Load sub. The next step in this task is to determine whether the user that is currently logged in is a technician, help desk manager, or general user. If you remember in Chapter 7, you created the clsUser class which contains a New sub to make this very determination. The code that we entered there set the Is Technician public property to True and the IsHelpDeskManager public property to False. Now that needs to be tested. Add the following code to the Page_Load sub within Default.aspx.vb:

```
Dim clsUser As New User(Session("UserLogin").ToString)
If clsUser.IsTechnician Or clsUser.IsHelpDeskManager Then
Response.Redirect("TechConsole.aspx")
Else
Response.Redirect("UserConsole.aspx")
End If
```

The first line of code declares an instance of the User class and passes the UserLogin value from the Session object as the userlogin parameter. Remember that the New sub within the User class sets the public properties IsTechnician and IsHelpDeskManager. Either one of those two types of users is directed to the Technician Console form.

The second line determines whether one of the two public properties of the User class is true.

The third line uses the Redirect method of the Request object to actually send the user to the TechConsole.aspx page. The Redirect method sends the user's browser to a new page that is provided as a parameter. In this case, the user will be sent to the TechConsole.aspx page.

The last three lines of code are the Else clause that is executed if the user fails both public property tests (meaning the user is a general user). General users are redirected to the User Console page instead of the Technician Console page.

The next step is to test this out. Start without debugging. You should see the Default.aspx web page appear and then immediately transfer to the TechConsole.aspx page. If you close the browser and start without debugging again, you probably won't see Default.aspx page appear at all, but instead see the Technician Console right off. The reason is that the first time the application is started the .NET Framework does a just-in-time compile of the forms and this may take several seconds. But, after the first loading of the application, it will load much more quickly and so the second time you'll only see the Technician Console page instead of the Default.aspx page first. This shows that the task has been tested successfully. The session object holds the user's login name and then passes it to the user class to determine if the user's login is a technician, help desk manager, or general user.

The next task is to add a button to the Technician Console that will allow help desk managers to access the administration forms for the application. This should be restricted to help desk managers only. To do this, the technician console page must be opened and the user must be examined again to determine their status of either technician or help desk manager. It's also possible for a user to jump into the middle of the application and figure out where the Technician Console is and therefore see tickets that they should not see. In the help desk application this is not a major issue. However, this task will also show how to redirect a user that may have jumped into the middle of your application.

The first step in this task is to open the Technician Console (TechConsole.aspx) page, add a button with an ID of btnAdministration, and then add a text of Administration. Next, view the code for the page or open TechConsole.aspx.vb from the Solution Explorer. The Page_Load sub should already exist and have code to assign the company name to the company name label. Within the Page_Load sub add

```
Dim clsuser As New User(Session("UserLogin").ToString)
If Not clsuser.IsHelpDeskManager Then
If Not clsuser.IsTechnician Then
Response.Redirect("UserConsole.aspx")
```

```
Else
btnAdministration.Visible = False
End If
Else
btnAdministration.Visible = True
End If
```

The first line of code will create a new instance of the User class and pass the value from the UserLogin session object as a parameter.

The second line will determine if the user is a help desk manager by checking the IsHelpDeskManager property of the User class.

The third line will only be executed if the user is not a help desk manager and will determine whether the user is a technician.

The fourth line will only be executed if the user is neither a technician nor a help desk manager. This line will redirect the user's browser to the User Console. This takes care of a user that may attempt to jump into the middle of the application without the correct security.

Line 6 will only be executed if the user is a technician and will set the visible property of the Administration button to false, making the Administration button invisible to the technician.

Line 9 will only be executed if the user is a help desk manager, and will set the visible property of the Administration button to true, making the Administration button visible to the help desk manager.

Now it is time to test this task. Start without debugging. The Technician Console page will appear, but the Administration button will not.

To test the scenario of the user being the help desk manager, open the clsUser.vb file and change the assignment statement blnIsHelpDeskManager = False within the New Sub to blnIsHelpDeskManager = True. The user will now be recognized as both a technician and a help desk manager and the Administration button should appear. Start without debugging again and the Technician Console will appear along with the Administration button.

Finally, to test the scenario where the user is neither a technician nor a help desk manager, change both lines within the New Sub in the User class to assign false. Start without debugging again. This time the User Console screen should appear instead of the Technician Console. This shows the redirect is working correctly for a user that is neither a technician nor a help desk manager.

The next task is to provide a form to allow users to add a new ticket. This includes adding a form, the necessary controls, and the code to provide the inputted values to the Ticket class. The first step is to create a new web form called AddTicket. On the form, add labels and text box controls for user login, first name, last name, phone number, location, e-mail address, problem description, and category. Also, add a button with an ID property of btnSave and a text property of Save. The completed form design should look like Figure 8-8.

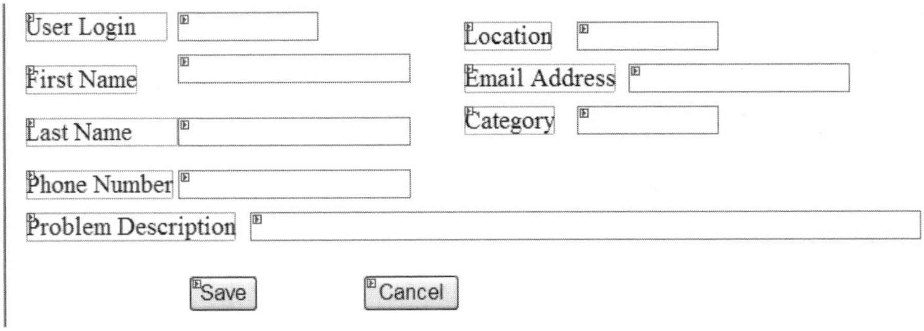

Figure 8-8. *Design View of Add Ticket web form*

Now that the form is laid out, it's time to add the code to save the ticket. To do this, double-click the Save button. This will open up the AddTicket.aspx.vb file and automatically create a Click event for the Save button. Before adding the necessary code to the click event, a variable of type Ticket class needs to be created. To do this, move to the top of the code page (just under the class name) and add Private clsTicket as Ticket. The class needs to be initiated within the Save click event and the information needs to be added from the form to the class. To do this, use the following code:

```
clsTicket = New Ticket
clsTicket.UserLogin = Trim(txtUserLogin.Text)
clsTicket.FirstName = Trim(txtFirstName.Text)
clsTicket.LastName = Trim(txtLastName.Text)
clsTicket.PhoneNumber = Trim(txtPhoneNumber.Text)
clsTicket.LocationID = Trim(txtLocation.Text)
clsTicket.EmailAddress = Trim(txtEmailAddress.Text)
clsTicket.Category = Trim(txtCategory.Text)
clsTicket.ProblemDescription = Trim(txtProblemDescription.Text)
```

The first line of code creates a new instance of the Ticket class and assigns it to the variable of type Ticket. The remaining lines assign the values from the form to the public properties of the Ticket class. Notice the use of the built-in Trim function. This function takes one parameter and returns a value that has stripped any blank spaces from the text. You should use this when passing data to a database. If, for example, the text box will hold 20 characters, and the user only types 5 but then presses the space bar 10 times, the value of the text property of the text box would still be 15 characters long. The Trim function would change that to only 5 characters long by removing the extra spaces.

You will probably also notice a squiggly line under txtlocation.text. The reason for this is that the public property of the Ticket class for location is expecting an integer. For now this is fine, but in Chapter 9 the location text box will be changed to a drop-down box, which will in turn provide a number value.

After adding the previous code, the public properties of the Ticket class have all been set. The next step is to call the NewTicket method of the Ticket class. When a user is adding an item, whatever that item might be, it's a good idea to let the user know that the information has been added. For that reason, open the AddTicket.aspx page again and add a label control with an ID property of lblStatus and a blank text property. This label will be used to let the user know whether the ticket was added or not and if the ticket was added what the ticket number was. Remember, the NewTicket method will return a Boolean value and the TicketID public property will contain the ID of the newly added ticket (this is hardcoded for now). Go back to the AddTicket.aspx.vb page and add

```
If clsTicket.NewTicket Then
lblStatus.Text = "Ticket added. Ticket number is " & clsTicket.TicketID
Else
lblStatus.Text = "Ticket was not added"
End If
```

to the end of the click event for the Save button.

The first line of code makes a call to the NewTicket method of the Ticket class. The NewTicket method is going to return either true or false. Based on the returned value, either line 2 or line 4 will be executed next. Notice line 2 includes the ticketid public property of the Ticket class.

The next step is to allow the user to cancel the inputted values and start again. To do this, add a new private sub called ClearValues within the AddTicket.aspx.vb file. Within the ClearValues sub set the text property of each control on the form to "" which will leave them blank. The code will look like

```
Private Sub ClearValues()
txtUserLogin.Text = string.empty
txtFirstName.Text = String.Empty
txtLastName.Text = String.Empty
txtPhoneNumber.Text = String.Empty
txtLocation.Text = String.Empty
txtEmailAddress.Text = String.Empty
txtCategory.Text = String.Empty
txtProblemDescription.Text = String.Empty
End Sub
```

The ClearValues sub needs to be called from the click event of the Cancel button. To do this, choose btnCancel (or your own name for the Cancel button) from the top left drop-down list and then choose Click from the top right drop-down list. The btnCancel_Click sub should appear. Within that sub, add the following line of code, ClearValues. When the Cancel button is clicked, the ClearValues sub will be called. This example also shows that the code for an event does not necessarily need to be within the event handlers declaration. You can also use this type of separation if you have a sub or function that needs to be called from multiple events. For example, you may want to clear all of the values on the form after the ticket is saved to allow the user to add another ticket immediately. Since you already have the ClearValues sub defined you would only need to call the ClearValues sub at the end of the click event for the Save button.

The last step in this task is to test the code. To do this, click on the AddTicket.aspx file in the Solution Explorer and choose Start without debugging from the Debug menu. Usually during the first test of a form, class, and, ultimately, database, I will type the name of the field into the text box so that I can make sure that each public property (and database column) is getting the correct value. For example, I would type User Login into the text box next to the User Login label. The only exception for this form is the location. Type **1** into the location field. The resulting test data should look like Figure 8-9.

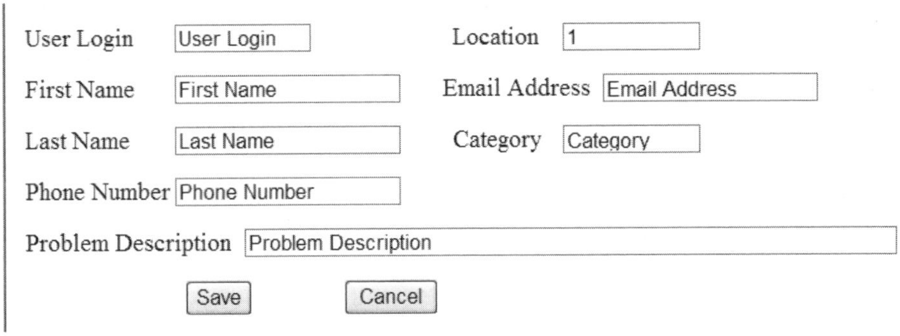

Figure 8-9. *Test data in AddTicket form*

After the test data is added, click the Save button. After the Save button has been clicked, the information from the form will be assigned to the public properties of the Ticket class and then the NewTicket method will be called. Also, within the NewTicket method the private function ValidateTicket will be called. You can verify this by adding a breakpoint to the first line of code within the Save button click event on the form and then debugging and stepping through the code. After the button is clicked, the label that was added should show that the ticket has been added and then give the ticket ID value of 10.

Also notice that the information entered is still within the text boxes. Again this is an example of the view state which holds the data for each control and posts it back to the form automatically, without the developer needing to do it specifically.

The last test to be conducted for this task would be to click the Cancel button. When you click the Cancel button all of the fields should be blanked out. Remember the click event of the Cancel button calls the ClearValues sub which assigns a blank value to the text property of each text control.

The last task for this chapter will be to make sure the validation of the public properties is correct and, if the validation fails, that the user is notified. Remember the NewTicket method of the Ticket class has a Try…Catch pair within it that throws any exceptions. Since the NewTicket method is called from the Save button's click event, the click event would receive any thrown exceptions and must be able to handle them.

To first show what happens when an exception is thrown but not handled, choose Start without debugging from the Debug menu. Enter a value for each field on the AddTicket.aspx form except the First Name text box (make sure you enter a number for location). Click the Save button. You will see a page that looks similar to Figure 8-10.

Server Error in '/HelpDesk' Application.

System.Exception: Errors have occured: First Name not provided
  at Ticket.ValidateTicket()
  at Ticket.NewTicket()

Description: An unhandled exception occurred during the execution of the current web request. Please review the stack the error and where it originated in the code.

Exception Details: System.Exception: System.Exception: Errors have occured: First Name not provided
  at Ticket.ValidateTicket()
  at Ticket.NewTicket()

Source Error:

The source code that generated this unhandled exception can only be shown whi
mode. To enable this, please follow one of the below steps, then request the

---

Figure 8-10. *Exception not handled*

This type of message is not very easy for a user to understand. So you'll need to add some exception handling to the Save button click event to handle any exceptions. To do this, add the word Try above the clsTicket = new Ticket line within the Save button click event. At the end of the code for the save button click event add

```
Catch ex As Exception
lblStatus.Text = ex.Message
End Try
```

This first line of code will catch any exceptions thrown from the code being executed. This catch statement will find any exceptions within the code that are between the try statement and this catch statement, including nested calls. Since the call to the NewTicket method of the Ticket class is between the Try and Catch statements, any exception thrown from the NewTicket method will be caught by this Catch statement. The second line of code assigns the message property of the exception to the text property of the label that is on the form. This will basically display the error message for the user to see.

To test this out, choose Start without debugging and then, when the form opens, again enter information for all fields except the First Name field (making sure to enter a number for location). This time a more readable message will appear, as shown in Figure 8-11, and the form will still be displayed.

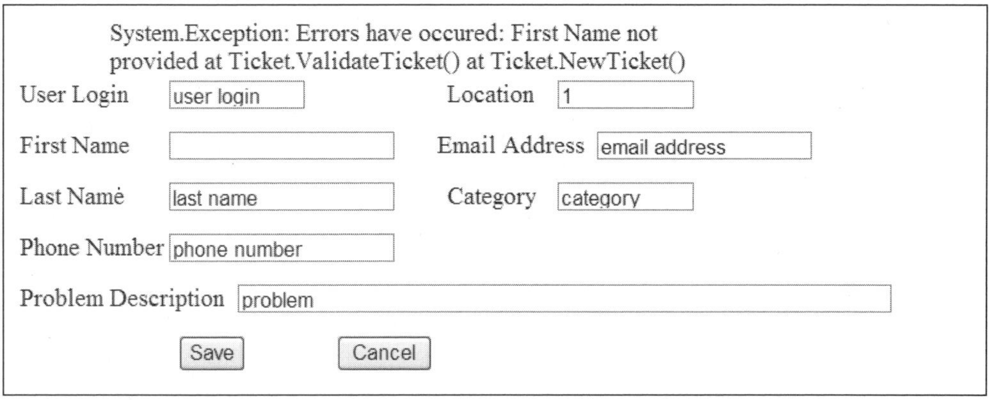

Figure 8-11. *New Exception message*

Now you know that the ValidateTicket method within the Ticket class is working correctly and that the exceptions are moved from the class code to the user interface.

Conclusion

In this chapter I provided an overview of the use of the Web Form Designer as well as an explanation of the life cycle of an ASP.NET page. I also expanded the Help Desk application you created in the previous chapter.

In the next chapter I'll provide more information about controls and use that information to improve the Help Desk application.

■ ■ ■

CHAPTER 9

ASP.NET Controls

In this chapter, I'll cover ASP.NET controls, which are used to create a user interface on a web form. After an introduction, I'll also expand on the Help Desk application from Chapter 8.

HTML Server Controls

HTML elements are not available to the server, because they are text that is passed through to the browser. HTML server controls are HTML elements (grouping of tags) that contain attributes that make them both visible to and programmable on the server. By creating HTML server controls and adding HTML elements to those controls, the HTML elements are exposed and can be programmed on the server. HTML attributes, such as Width for the <td> tag, are exposed in an HTML server control as a property (properties will be covered later in this chapter).

Any HTML element on a page can be converted to an HTML server control. To make an HTML element a server control, add the attribute RUNAT="SERVER", as in the following examples.

HTML Input element:

```
<input id="Button1" type="button" value="button" />
```

HTML Input server control:

```
<input id="Button1" type="button" value="button" runat="server" />
```

The runat attribute tells the ASP.NET page framework that it should create an instance of the control for server-side page processing. You can also use the form designer to change an HTML element into a server control. To show this, open the Help Desk application you previously created and then open the TechConsole.aspx page. Within the Toolbox, find the HTML section of the Toolbox as shown in Figure 9-1. To find the HTML Section, you may need to scroll up or down the Toolbox. The HTML section of the Toolbox will have a title of HTML.

Figure 9-1. *HTML section of the toolbox*

Drag and drop the Input (Button) HTML element from the toolbox onto the TechConsole.aspx page. After dragging the element onto the form, click the Source button at the bottom of the Designer, if you are not already in Source mode (see Chapter 8 for more instructions). The HTML source for the page will appear, as shown in Figure 9-2.

```
 1  <%@ Page Language="VB" AutoEventWireup="false" CodeFile="TechConsole.a

 2

 3  <!DOCTYPE html PUBLIC "-//W3C//DTD XHTML 1.1//EN" "http://www.w3.org/T

 4

 5  <html xmlns="http://www.w3.org/1999/xhtml" >

 6  <head runat="server">

 7      <title>Untitled Page</title>

 8  </head>

 9  <body>

10      <form id="form1" runat="server">

11      <div>

12          <asp:Label ID="lblPageName" runat="server" Style="z-index: 100

13              top: 40px" Text="Technician Console" Width="168px"></asp:L

14

15          <asp:Label ID="lblCompanyName" runat="server" Style="z-index:

16              top: 8px" Width="216px"></asp:Label>

17          <asp:Button ID="btnAdministration" runat="server" Style="z-ind

18              top: 64px" Text="Administration" />

19          <input id="Button1" style="z-index: 103; left: 24px; position:

20              type="button" value="button" />

21

22      </div>

23      </form>

24  </body>
```

Figure 9-2. *Source for HTML Input element*

Notice that there is an HTML tag that begins with asp:Button. This tag is for the Administration button that was placed on TechConsole.aspx previously. The tag that begins with input is the HTML element that was just placed there. Also notice the asp:Button tag has a runat attribute with a value of "server", while the input tag does not. This tells the .NET Framework that this is a server control.

To convert this HTML element to an HTML server control, which can then be used at the server, click on the Design button at the bottom of the Designer to move back to Design mode. After doing this, right-click on the HTML Input button on the form and then choose Run As Server Control, as shown in Figure 9-3.

This will add the necessary attribute to the HTML element, in order to make the element a server control, and therefore allow it to be executed from the server. Click the Source button at the bottom of the Designer again to view the updated HTML element. The revised source includes the runat attribute, as shown in Figure 9-4.

Figure 9-3. *Choosing Run As Server Control*

```
 9 <body>
10     <form id="form1" runat="server">
11         <div>
12             <asp:Label ID="lblPageName" runat="server" Style="z-index: 100
13                 top: 40px" Text="Technician Console" Width="168px"></asp:L
14
15             <asp:Label ID="lblCompanyName" runat="server" Style="z-index:
16                 top: 8px" Width="216px"></asp:Label>
17             <asp:Button ID="btnAdministration" runat="server" Style="z-ind
18                 top: 64px" Text="Administration" />
19             <input id="Button1" style="z-index: 103; left: 24px; position:
20                 type="button" value="button" runat="server" />
21
22         </div>
23     </form>
24 </body>
```

Figure 9-4. *Revised HTML element with runat attribute*

Notice the tag is still an Input tag, not an asp:Button tag. This is because the HTML element is being run at the server instead of being a full-blown server control. After adding the runat attribute, you can reference a control within your code if you assign an ID attribute to it. In this example the ID is Button1. I'll cover working with the methods and properties of a control, along with a description of the property differences between an HTML element and a standard sever control later in this chapter.

Web Server Controls

Web server controls are similar to HTML server controls, except the web server control does not map directly to an HTML server control. The HTML rendered by the control may be different than what you write program code to interact with. When you're using the HTML server control, you can change and program the exact HTML attributes. But with the web server control you are dealing with properties and methods of the control, which in turn generates the necessary HTML attributes and tags. Web server controls include normal form controls, such as buttons and text boxes, as well as controls that can display data in grids and choose a date.

Web server controls also provide a more complete object model and automatic browser detection, in order to determine the best output for a browser. Some controls include the ability to define a customized look for the control through the use of a template. Also, some controls allow you to determine whether the events on the control cause an immediate postback to the server or instead wait for the form to be submitted.

As shown in both Figure 9-3 and Figure 9-4, the web server controls all begin their tags with asp: followed by the type of control they represent (button, textbox, and so on). When the page runs, the web server control is rendered to the page using appropriate HTML. The control determines which HTML to render, based on the browser type and the settings that have been provided as properties for the control.

Working with Control Properties and Events

Both HTML server controls and web server controls allow you to manipulate some of the attributes of the HTML to be rendered, as well as defining what happens when events occur. There is a large difference between properties that can be changed for an HTML server control, shown in Figure 9-5, and the properties that can be changed for a web server control, shown in Figure 9-6.

In Figure 9-5 notice the limited properties that can be changed. These are a direct match to the possible HTML attributes for a button. In Figure 9-6, the list of properties is much richer in features and goes well beyond the possible HTML attributes for a button.

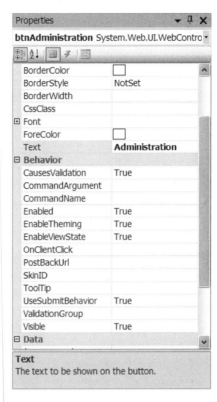

Figure 9-6. *Web server control properties*

Change the ID property of the new HTML button control to btnAddNew. Notice there isn't a text property for the HTML button control. Instead there is a value property. The value property of an HTML control is the same as the Text property of a server control. Change the Value property of the same control to New Ticket.

Click the Administration button and view the Properties window. Again, notice the number of properties that can be changed. These properties are broken down into categories. The first is Accessibility, which are the properties that can be used to make the button accessible through the keyboard as well as the tab index. You can use the Tab Index property of each control on a form to set the order in which controls are given focus when the Tab key is used. This allows the user to tab through the controls. You should incorporate this functionality when doing a data entry form (like AddTicket.aspx), so that the user can enter information using the keyboard and then tab to the next control, where they can enter more information, and continue that cycle.

The next category of properties is Appearance. Use these properties to determine how the control will look to the user. This includes the background and foreground color as well as font. You can change the font by expanding the font section within this category. Many of the common fonts are listed in a drop-down list. You can also choose the size of the font and whether the font should be in bold or italics or neither. When choosing a font, be careful to choose a common font. Be aware that some browsers may not support certain types of fonts, so it is a good idea to use the most common fonts, such as Arial and Times New Roman.

The next category of properties is Behavior. This category contains properties that determine some action or behavior of the control. This includes the enabled property, which can be used to either enable or disable a control. A disabled control will appear gray on the screen and the user will not be able to interact with it, either by clicking it, if it's a button, or by typing in a text box. The Visible property determines whether the control can be seen or not. As shown in the previous chapter there are cases when you may want to show a button (visible = true) when a certain criterion is met, but then not show the button (visible = false) when that criterion is not met. The Tooltip property within this section can be used to display a message when the mouse is over the control. This can be used to give directions to a user or to provide a name for a control that a user can understand.

The next category of properties is Data. For a button control, this property can be used to bind a certain value to the text property. It can also be used to assign a configuration or application setting to the text property, so that it can be changed later. You can use configuration and application files and settings to hold text that will be assigned to the text property of a control. This way that text value can be changed when necessary without having to recompile and redeploy the application. (Compiling and redeploying are outside the scope of this book.)

The next category of properties is Layout. There are two properties here, height and width. You can use these properties to define a default height and width for the control instead of resizing the control manually on the screen. If you want all of the controls to be the same size you could use this to make sure they are all the same size.

The last category of properties is Misc. This category will list any properties that did not fit into the other categories. For the Administration button the only property here is the ID property. The ID property is the name of the control to be used in code. By default each control has a name based on the control type and how many of those controls exist on the same form. You can't have more than one control on the same page with the same name. If you attempt to do this, you will receive an error message when you move away from the Properties window.

Not all server controls have the same properties. This is the advantage to using web server controls versus HTML controls. The web server controls have been built to generate the necessary HTML for a set of properties and therefore have been customized for that type of control. If you click the label "Technician Console" on the TechConsole.aspx page and view the properties you will notice the list of properties is slightly different. For example the label control does not have a Causesvalidation property and some other properties within the Behavior category. The reason is these properties are not relevant to the label control. They are relevant to the button control and some others but not the label.

Both HTML and web server controls have events as well as properties. You can view the events for either type of control by being both in the Designer and in Design mode (not Source mode), right-clicking, and then choosing View Code. You can write code to be executed each time one of these events occurs by choosing the server control and then the event. The events do vary based on the type of control (HTML versus web server control). For example, right-click the TechConsole.aspx page anywhere on the form and choose View Code. From the top left drop-down list choose btnAddNew. From the top right drop-down list choose ServerClick. This will create a server click event for btnAddNew. Notice there is already a Click event for btnAdministration. Again the difference is that btnAddNew is an HTML control. Within the ServerClick event of the btnAddNew control type `Response.Redirect("AddTicket.aspx")`. This will redirect the browser to AddTicket.aspx when the New Ticket button is clicked.

Validation Controls

Validation controls are controls that include logic that allows you to test a user's input. Validation controls can be used to check for a required field, test against a specific value or pattern, verify that entered data falls within a range, as well as for allowing custom validation.

To show this in action, you are going to add validation controls to the AddTicket.aspx page within the Help Desk application. Save the changes you've made to the TechConsole.aspx page and close it. Then, open the AddTicket.aspx page. To use a validation control, find the Validation section of the toolbox, as shown in Figure 9-7.

From the Toolbox choose the RequiredFieldValidator control and drag it next to the User Login text box on the AddTicket.aspx (you may need to move other controls around). The resulting Design View is shown in Figure 9-8.

Next, view the properties for the control, shown in Figure 9-9.

There are two properties that you should look for. The first is the Error Message property, which is the property that controls the error message that will be displayed. Enter **User Login is required** in the Error Message Property box.

The second property is the ControlToValidate property. This property provides a drop-down list of all the possible controls that you can validate on the form, as shown in Figure 9-10.

Figure 9-7. *Validation section of the Toolbox*

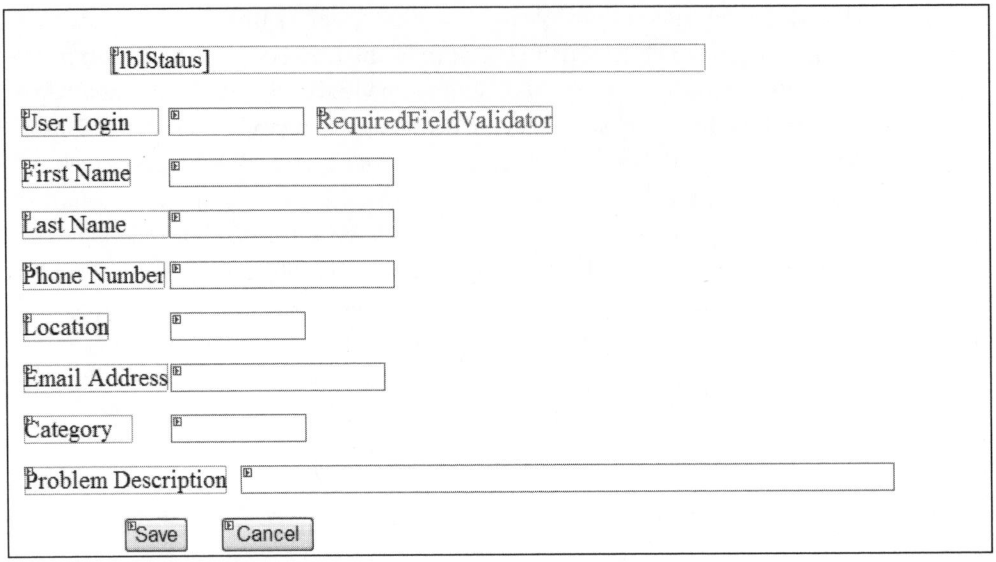

[lblStatus]

User Login   □   RequiredFieldValidator

First Name   □

Last Name   □

Phone Number □

Location   □

Email Address □

Category   □

Problem Description □

[Save] [Cancel]

Figure 9-8. *Form after RequiredFieldValidator control added*

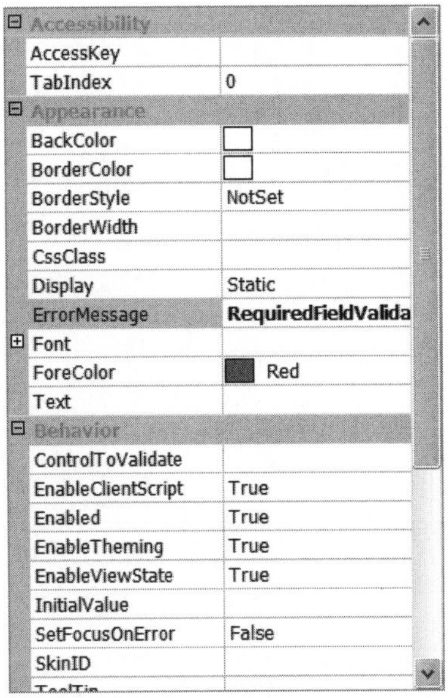

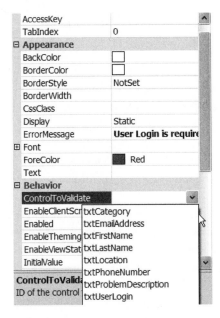

Figure 9-9. *Validation control properties*

Figure 9-10. *ControlToValidate property*

Next, choose txtUserLogin from the list. Also, change the ID property to UserLoginRequired. Now, to show how the validation control works, choose Start without Debugging from the Debug menu. Do not enter any values for any of the fields and then click the Save button. You'll see text appear next to the User Login text box, which matches the ErrorMessage property of the validation control, as shown in Figure 9-11.

User Login		User Login is required
First Name		
Last Name		
Phone Number		
Location		
Email Address		
Category		
Problem Description		
Save	Cancel	

Figure 9-11. *Validation message returned*

You'll notice that the error message stating that none of the values were provided was not displayed, as it was in the same situation in Chapter 8. The reason for this is that the validation control is fired prior to the code for the button event. Therefore, this validation occurs before any of the code in the click event of the Save button is run. This is a good way to make sure that the user sees any errors before they move off the page. This also saves round trip (transfer to the server and back) work as your code on the server, within the Ticket class, is never executed because the error is found at the client instead of the server.

The RangeValidator control is another useful validation control. This control can be used to verify that your values are within acceptable ranges. For example, if you want a user to enter a value that should be between 1 and 10, this control will display an error message if the value is outside of that range.

To show this, drag and drop the RangeValidator control to the AddTicket.aspx page and then place it next to the Location text box control. For now, the Location control is gathering a number and passing it to an integer public property of the Ticket class. Click on the RangeValidator control and view the properties. Change the ErrorMessage property to Location is out of Range, change the control to validate to txtLocation, and change the ID property to LocationRange. Notice that there is a MaximumValue and MinimumValue property. These are the lowest and highest values that can be entered into the validated control. Enter 1 as the MinimumValue and 10 as the MaximumValue.

Another useful validation control is the RegularExpressionValidator. This control can be used to verify that the fields have the correct type of information entered, whether phone number, zip code, or e-mail address. The control does this by making sure that the information entered into the control matches the pattern for each of these types of values. To use this control, drag and drop the RegularExpressionValidator control to the AddTicket.aspx form, next to the Email Address text box. Set the ErrorMessage property to Email Address is not valid, and the ID property to EmailMailExpression. Set the Controltovalidate property to Txtemailaddress. Also, notice that there is a Validationexpression property. Click the ellipses next to this property to get a box that allows you to choose which expression to use. When you find the one called Internetemailaddress, choose it.

To test out the validation controls, choose Start without debugging from the Debug menu. This time enter any value for User Login, enter **15** into the Location text box, and then tab off the text box. You will get an error message, telling you that the Location is not in range, immediately. Type **emailaddress** into the e-mail address text box and then tab off. This time you'll get the Email Address is not valid error message immediately.

You can use all of the validation controls that I've covered to give the user feedback as quickly as possible.

Master Pages

Master pages allow you to create a consistent look for all pages within an application. A single master page defines a standard look and feel for either a group of pages or an entire application. Individual content pages can contain specific content as needed though—when a user requests the individual content page it's merged with the master page to produce the output. A master page has a file extension of .master and has a predefined layout that includes static text, HTML elements, and/or server controls. Master pages allow centralized common functionality, which allows you to make updates in one place, use one set of controls and code for multiple pages, and allow you to control the layout of the final page by giving you control of the placeholders.

To try this out, you're going to add a master page to the Help Desk application.

First, add a new master page, the same way that you would add any new form. Give your page the name HD.Master (the default extension of a master page). Next, you're going to add a company logo to the master page so that it appears on each page. To do this, you need to copy the image file that you want to use into the same folder as your web site (most likely c:\inetpub\wwwroot\HelpDesk). After the image file is within the web site folder, click the web site URL within the Solution Explorer and choose Add Existing Item. When the Add Existing Item window appears, choose the image file. Now that the image is within the project structure, place your cursor at the top of the master page and press enter a couple of times. This will move the contentplaceholder control down the page. The contentplaceholder is a control that will hold the content that you want to create for the child pages. After the contentplaceholder is moved, click and drag the image file from the Solution Explorer to the top left corner of the master page. Add a label with an ID of lblCompanyName and do not add a text property. The results should look like Figure 9-12.

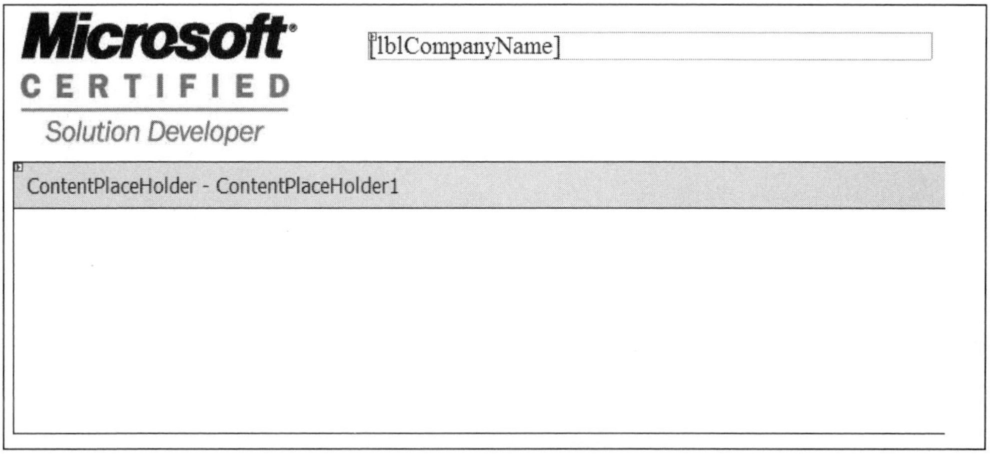

Figure 9-12. *Design of master page, HD.master*

The master page is now complete. The problem is that you can't associate a master page with an existing page. So, each of the pages that you've already created will need to be re-created to be used with the master page. For now though, you're only going to create new pages to work alongside your master page.

Next add a new web form called ViewTickets to the web site. When the Add New Item window appears, check the box Select master page, as shown in Figure 9-13.

When you click the Add button, the Select a Master Page window will appear. All master pages within the web site will also appear. Select the master page you want associated with this web form (in this case HD.master), and click OK, as shown in Figure 9-14.

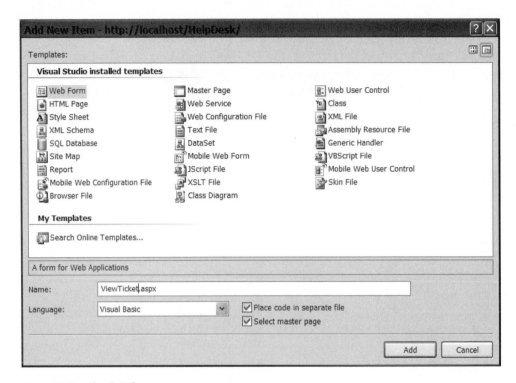

Figure 9-13. *Check Select master page*

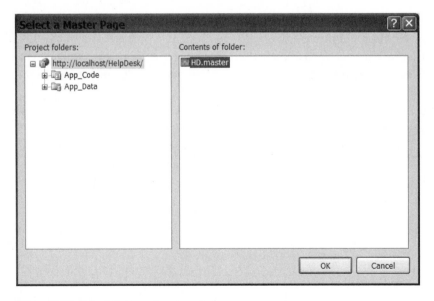

Figure 9-14. *Select the master page to use*

You'll notice the layout of the master page can be seen when the new page is opened, but that the master page content is grayed out, as shown in Figure 9-15.

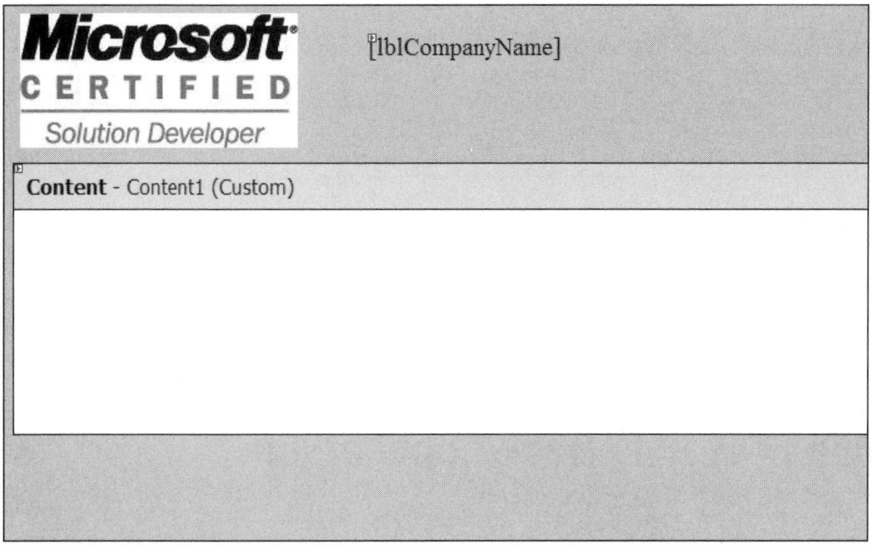

Figure 9-15. *ViewTicket.aspx with grayed out master page content*

Next, drag and drop a label from the toolbox onto the ViewTicket page. Set the ID property to lblTicketID and the text property to Ticket ID. Drag and drop a text box from the toolbox onto the ViewTicket page and then set the ID property to txtTicketID. You'll use these properties to show how the content page works.

You can also make sure that all the pages that use the master page get the same code, by adding this code to the master page. This is a useful strategy for doing something like populating the company name label on each page at once, rather than adding the code to do this on each individual page.

To do this, open the HD.master.vb file. Choose Page Events from the top left drop-down list and then choose load from the top right drop-down list. This will create the page load sub.

Within the page load sub add

```
lblCompanyName.Text = Application("CompanyName").ToString
```

This code will be executed each time a page that is associated with the master page is loaded. To see this in action, click the ViewTicket.aspx page again and choose Start without debugging from the Debug menu. The resulting page will look similar to Figure 9-16.

Figure 9-16. *ViewTicket.aspx file showing content and master file*

Notice that both the master page content and the ViewTicket.aspx page content are present and that the name of the company was loaded when the master page was loaded.

Expanding the Help Desk Application

In this section I'll take the existing Help Desk application and use some of the information I've presented in this chapter to add more to the web site. This will include setting the tab order for fields, making the problem description field a multiple line text box, changing fonts, aligning controls, and using drop-down lists.

Your first task is to order the tabs of the controls on the AddTicket.aspx page. The reason you should order the controlsy is so that the user entering information into your form can tab from one control to the next. The flow of your controls should be logical and follow the most common order—for example, your State field should follow your City field, rather than the other way around. Only controls that require user interaction such as buttons or text boxes should have a value in their tab index property.

To do this, open AddTicket.aspx and click the User Login control. Next, view the properties page for the control. Then, find the tab index property and enter **1**. You should always start the tab order with 1. Click on the FirstName text box and change the tab index to **2**. Repeat this for all of the text boxes and then do the same for the buttons. The Save button should have a tab index before the Cancel button.

Tip When working with the properties of multiple controls you might find it useful to pin the Properties window open. To do this, click the icon that looks like a pin at the top of the Properties window (it will say Auto Hide when you mouse over it). Clicking the pin should point it downwards instead of sideways. This will keep the Properties window visible, rather than hidden, when you're not working with it.

When you have added the tab index to each control, it's time to test your work! Start without debugging. Then, click the mouse into the first text box and hit the Tab key.

When the Tab key is hit, the cursor should move to the next text box. Continue doing this until you reach the Cancel button. If hitting the tab key did result in the correct text box getting the cursor, verify the tab index property of the controls in question.

Your next task is to make a problem description field with multiple lines. The default behavior of a text box control is to only accept one line of text, which means under normal circumstances you can't hit the Enter key and that you have limited space for typing.

For example, while you have the AddTicket.aspx file open, type something into the Problem Description text box. Continue typing until you reach the end of the text box. You will notice that what you have already typed will scroll to the left, and that this will continue to happen as you continue to type.

To fix this problem, you can set the text box control's Textmode property set to Multiline. To do this, close the web site and open the AddTicket.aspx page. First, expand the Problem Description text box so that it's wider. Next, view the properties for the Problem Description text box and find the Textmode property. Click the drop-down list and choose Multiline. This will allow the text box to accept multiple lines of text and will also allow the user to hit Enter. This will also allow your user to view all of the content at once, until the content is below the bottom of the text box.

When there is more content than can be viewed within the text box, scroll bars will automatically appear. To see this happen, start without debugging and enter a large amount of text into the Problem Description text box, as shown in Figure 9-17.

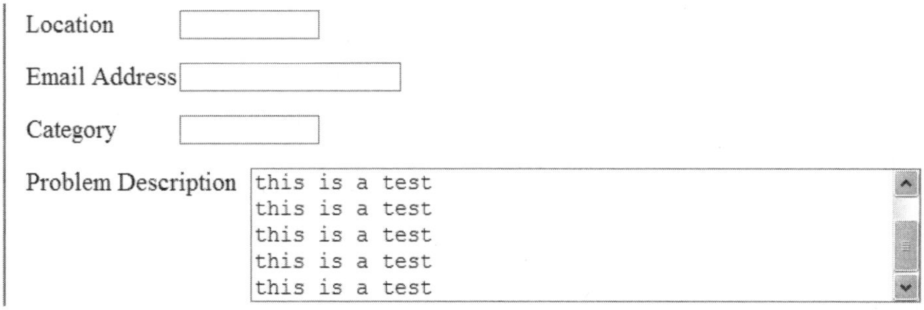

Figure 9-17. *Multiline text box with scroll bars*

Notice that not only are the scroll bars present, but also that there are multiple lines of text. You can't see from Figure 9-17, but there is a carriage return (made using the Enter key) at the end of each line. This can't be done in a single line text box.

Your next task is to change the font of all of the label controls. First, click each label while holding down the Control key. This will allow you to select all of the labels at one time. Next view the Properties window and find the Font property under the appearance category. Click the + sign next to the font property to expand the set. From there, click the drop-down list next to the Name property. This is the Font Name property. Choose Arial from the list. Next, find the Size property within the Font set and use the drop-down menu to choose Small. The resulting properties window is shown in Figure 9-18.

While you have all of the labels selected, you can also choose to align all of the labels. To do this, choose the Format menu and Align, and then Lefts, as shown in Figure 9-19.

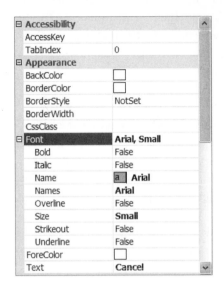

Figure 9-18. *Font properties*   **Figure 9-19.** *Align Lefts*

This technique can be used to align any set of controls. As you can see from the menu, you can align the lefts, centers, rights, tops, middles, and bottoms of a set of controls. All you need to do is just select the controls you want to align by holding down the Control button and clicking on the controls that you want to include in the grouping.

Your final task is to change the Location text box to a drop-down list. A drop-down list can be loaded dynamically from a database, manually added within the Properties window, or item by item via added code. Again, since ADO.NET is outside the scope of this book, you will only be adding items from the Properties window and then with code.

The first step is to remove the Location text box and then drag and drop a drop-down list control from the toolbox. When you drag the drop-down list control onto the form, you'll see a small box with two tasks listed, as shown in Figure 9-20.

You can click on the first task, if you are using ADO.NET, to determine where the data for the list should come from. You can choose the second task to add items to the list manually through the Property window. The check box at the end of the list determines whether you want the drop-down list to force the page to refresh (postback) when you select an item from the drop-down list. For the Help Desk

Figure 9-20. *Drop-down list tasks*

application this isn't necessary. However, you could use this to post back the results of the drop-down list if that specific information is needed for another control on the form. For example, if one drop-down list depended on another, you could enable the Autopostback control for the first drop-down list and then populate the second drop-down list on page load, if there was a postback.

Click the Edit Items task to manually add the items to the drop-down list. When the ListItem Collection Editor window appears click the Add button. This will add an item to the list and allow you to manipulate some of the properties of the list item as shown in Figure 9-21.

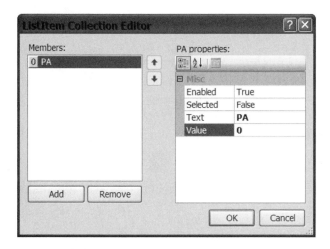

Figure 9-21. *ListItem Collection Editor after Add*

The first property on the list determines whether the list item is enabled or not (grayed out). The second property determines whether the item is selected when the list is first shown. Only one item can have the Selected property set to True.

The third and fourth properties are the most important. The third property is the text to be displayed, while the fourth property is the value that will be provided when the item is selected. Enter **PA** as the text and **0** (zero) as the value. Next, add another list item with a text of **NY** and a value of **1.** Finally, add a third list item with a text of **NJ** and a value of **2.**

You'll also notice a Remove button. You can use this button to remove an existing list item. Just click on the list item you want to remove, and then click the Remove button. When you have added all three items, click OK and then move the drop-down list next to the Location label.

■Note The Text and Value properties of a list item are represented as strings. Either one can contain alphanumeric values. If you wanted to, you could use PA as both the text and the value. In this case, the class Ticket is expected an integer value, so 0 (zero) was assigned to the value.

To test this out, first delete the Rangevalidator control that is associated with the Location text box. Since the text box is no longer on the page, the validation control will cause an error when building the web site. Also, the drop-down list guarantees that the values for the location are valid. Since the text box doesn't exist anymore, the value from the text box control can't be determined. This means you also need to change the code that assigns the value from the Location text box control to the Location Public property within the Ticket class. To do this, double-click the Save button, which will bring you to the Button save click event. You will now see a line of code with a squiggly line under it, which will be the line that assigns the text property of the Location text box to the Location Public property of the Ticket class:

```
clsTicket.LocationID = txtLocation.Text.Trim()
```

For now, place a single quote before this line, which will comment the line out. (All of the characters will be green in a commented-out line.) A commented line of code will not be executed when the other code is executed. You will also find a reference to txtlocation in the ClearValues sub. Place a single quote before that line to comment it out also.

Next, choose Start without debugging from the Debug menu. The AddTicket page will appear and you will see the drop-down list, as shown in Figure 9-22.

Notice that PA is the selected item. PA is the first item in the list so it's automatically selected.

The next step is to assign the value from the drop-down list to the location property of the Ticket class. To do this, close the web site and view AddTicket.aspx in Design Mode again. Click on the drop-down list and view its properties. Change the ID property to DDLocation. Double-click the Save button to go to the Button save click event. Remove the single quote that was used to comment out the line of code assigning the public property of the Ticket class. Remove the assignment part of the statement:

Figure 9-22. *AddTicket.aspx with drop-down list for location*

```
trim(txtlocation.text)
```

Next, type DDLocation followed by a period. This will show you all of the various drop-down list properties and methods that are available to you. Find the property called SelectedValue and then select it. The SelectedValue property of a drop-down control holds the value property of the selected item. Your code will look like

```
clsTicket.LocationID = cint(ddlocation.SelectedValue)
```

The cint built-in function will convert the string value from the SelectedValue property to an integer required for the public property LocationID of the Ticket class.

To test this out, place a breakpoint on the line of code that was just changed (the location assignment line). Then, choose Start debugging from the Debug menu. You will receive the error message that is shown in Figure 9-23. Never fear—this message just enables debugging. Click OK to continue.

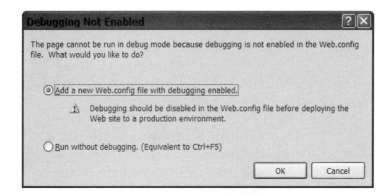

Figure 9-23. *Debugging not enabled message*

Enter a value for each of the fields, and be sure to put in a valid e-mail address. Choose NY from the drop-down list and then click Save. When the breakpoint is hit, place your mouse over the cint(DDLocation.SelectedValue) statement. You will see that the value is 1. Remember that the list item with a text of NY had a value of 1 so you know that this is correct. You can now stop the execution of the web site.

The final step in this task is to add an item programmatically. I like to add an item to the beginning of the list that lets the user know what to select. For example, in this case I would add "Select a Location" to the list. To do this, create a new private sub called AddItem within the AddTicket.aspx.vb file. First, you need to declare a variable of type New ListItem called NItem. The ListItem object represents one item in a list. Next, set the Text property of the NItem object to "Select a location", set the value property of the NItem object to "999", and set the Selected property of the NItem object to True. Finally, you must add the NItem object to the drop-down list's items collection. To do that use DDLocation.Items.Add(NItem). This line of code calls the Add method of the Items collection for the drop-down list. The finished sub will look like this:

```
Private Sub AddItem()
Dim NItem As New ListItem
NItem.Text = "Select a Location"
NItem.Value = "999"
NItem.Selected = True
DDLocation.Items.Add(NItem)
End Sub
```

Next, a call to this sub must be placed in the Page Load event. To do this, choose Page Events from the top left drop-down list and then choose Load from the top right drop-down list. Within the Page Load event enter **AddItem**. This will call the AddItem sub when the page is first loaded. To test this, choose Start without debugging from the Debug menu. The resulting page will look like Figure 9-24.

Figure 9-24. *AddTicket with Select a Location item added*

Notice that the Select a Location item is the one that is visible. That's because the Selected property was set to True. If you use the drop-down list, you'll see that Select a Location is last in the list. This is because the Value property of the list item was set to 999, so it will be last in the list and will be out of the range for the value.

Now all of the new controls and features have been added to the Help Desk application. The next chapter will use a web service to retrieve information about the requester.

Conclusion

In this chapter, I explained the difference between the various ASP.NET controls that can be used on a web form. I also covered how to use the properties of ASP.NET controls and how to use a master page to define the layout of all the pages within an application. Finally, I expanded on the Help Desk application that we started previously, by adding controls and setting properties for those controls. In the next chapter I'll cover what a web service is and how to implement a very simple web service.

CHAPTER 10

Web Services

In this chapter, I'll introduce you to XML, SOAP, WSDL, and web services. I'll also explain how to create a web service and then deploy that web service. I'll expand on the Help Desk application by showing you how to create a web service to retrieve user information and then add code to use this web service.

Introduction to XML, SOAP, and WSDL

XML, or Extensible Markup Language, is a markup language that provides a format for describing data. XML is similar to HTML in that both are markup languages and both use the concept of a tag. However, XML only has a handful of standard tags, and you can also create your own tags, which you can't do with HTML. Also, XML tags are used to define the structure and the data types of the data itself. As I just mentioned, the advantage of XML is that you can create your own tags to describe your data. XML is used mostly to move data between different systems when the two systems involved don't need to understand how the data was created. Unlike a comma delimited file, an XML file is grouped by the XML tags and doesn't need to be in the same order all of the time. For more information about XML, check out the XML Developer Center at `http://msdn.Microsoft.com/xml`.

SOAP is a simple, XML-based protocol for exchanging structured and type information on the web. This protocol is highly modular and extensible. Web services use the SOAP protocol, which is similar to TCP/IP and HTTP, to communicate with clients. The SOAP messages sent to and from a web service must be in XML with a required Body and Envelope element and an optional Header element.

WSDL stands for Web Services Description Language, which is an XML grammar that is used to create an XML document. The XML document created by WSDL is a service description that describes a web service and defines the format of messages that the web service understands. The service description serves as an agreement that defines the behavior of a web service and instructs potential clients on how to interact with the service. The WSDL specification can be found at `http://www.w3.org/TR/wsdl`.

Introduction to Web Services

Web services have received plenty of attention in the past few years. A *web service* is essentially an application that can be accessed by other applications via the web. Usually web services provide small amounts of functionality that are specific. One example of a web service would be a mailing address verifier. This kind of web service would have the functionality to determine whether a mailing address is in the correct format. In practice, the web service might receive a request via HTTP (internet protocol) that contains a mailing address. The web service would then perform the work to determine whether the mailing address was valid and would return either a true or false value, depending on the outcome. The advantage to a web service is that it is loosely coupled and can be reached over the internet. *Loosely coupled* means that the two systems (the web service and the client) only need to understand self-describing, text-based messages (XML). A company could use a web service to provide invoice information to customers very similar to the EDI (Electronic Data Interchange).

To use the functionality of a web service, a client application must exist. This client application can be a Windows client or a web client. The client application must reference the web service and must understand what to present to the web service and what the web service will return.

Creating a Web Service

To show you how a web service is created and then used, you're going to create a web service, called UserInformation. The UserInformation web service will provide user information for other applications. In this case, it will be used by the Help Desk application to provide information about a user. In real life, this could be used as a way to retrieve user information about all users for all applications within a company. The web service could interact with either a database or a directory service like Active Directory to provide this information. The advantage is that you can build one web service and use it for multiple applications, instead of needing to include the classes necessary to retrieve user data in either a namespace for the company to use or in each individual application.

The first step in creating a web service is to install Internet Information Service (IIS) on the local computer. If you do not have IIS installed, you will not be able to create a web service. If you do have IIS installed, open Visual Studio 2005 and choose File ➤ New Web Site. In the New Web Site window, choose ASP.NET Web Service and enter **UserInformation** as the name of the web service, as shown in Figure 10-1.

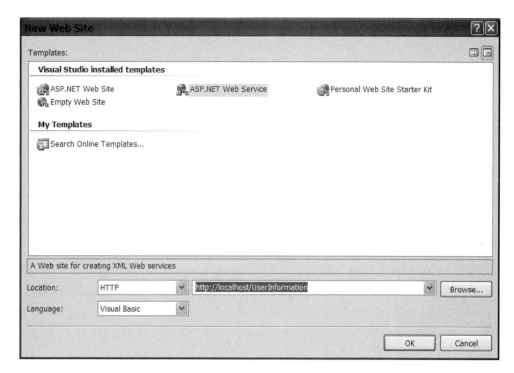

Figure 10-1. *Entering UserInformation as the new application name*

When the project opens, a file called Service.vb will be automatically created and displayed. You can close this window. Next, open the Solution Explorer, find the file called Service.asmx, and delete it along with the Service.vb file. After deleting those two files, right-click on the URL at the top of the Solution Explorer and choose Add New Item. When the Add New Item window appears, choose Web Service and then give it the name UserInformation. A vb file is also created with the code itself. Now, open the UserInformation.vb file. The first line after the Imports line is a line that starts with WebService. Change that line so that it's the same as Figure 10-2.

```
<WebService(Namespace:="http://localhost/UserInformation", _
    Description:="Retrieve user information.")> _
<WebServiceBinding(ConformsTo:=WsiProfiles.BasicProfile1_1)> _
```

Figure 10-2. *Updated UserInformation.vb file*

This changes the namespace from the default name and adds a description that can be viewed by a user of the web service. There are several different items of information about a user. For each item, a method will be defined. Use the following code to define each method (GetFirstName, GetLastName, GetPhoneNumber, GetEmailAddress, GetLocation):

```
<WebMethod(Description:="Retrieves the First Name of the user")> _
 Public Function GetFirstName(ByVal UserLogin As String) As Boolean
 End Function
```

The first line of the previous code declares this as a WebMethod and provides a description of the method for users of the web service. The WebMethod line of code must be entered prior to any method that is to be exposed as part of the web service. After the WebMethod line, any function or sub can be written. Within each method, determine whether the login is equal to the login that you are going to test within. If it is, return a value—otherwise return an empty string. The resulting code should look like this:

```
<WebMethod(Description:="Get the first name for the user")> _
Public Function GetFirstName(ByVal UserLogin As String) As String
If UserLogin = "Brian" Then
Return "Brian"
Else
Return ""
End If
End Function
<WebMethod(Description:="Get the last name for the user")> _
Public Function GetLastName(ByVal UserLogin As String) As String
If UserLogin = "Brian" Then
Return "Myers"
Else
Return ""
End If
End Function
<WebMethod(Description:="Get the phone number for the user")> _
Public Function GetPhoneNumber(ByVal UserLogin As String) As String
If UserLogin = "Brian" Then
Return "555-5555"
Else
Return ""
End If
End Function
<WebMethod(Description:="Get the email address for the user")> _
Public Function GetEmailAddress(ByVal UserLogin As String) As String
If UserLogin = "Brian" Then
Return "email@company.com"
Else
Return ""
End If
```

```
End Function
<WebMethod(Description:="Get the location id for the user")> _
Public Function GetLocation(ByVal UserLogin As String) As Integer
If UserLogin = "Brian" Then
Return 2
Else
Return 0
End If
End Function
```

To test this out, switch to the Test.asmx file and execute the application (Debug ➤ Start without debugging). The .asmx file will appear and display the available methods for the service, along with a description of each, as shown in Figure 10-3.

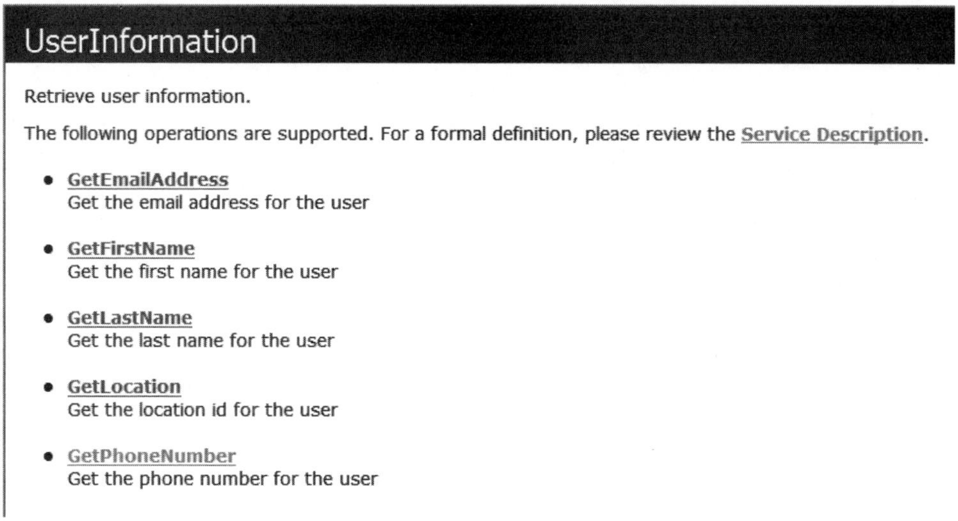

UserInformation

Retrieve user information.

The following operations are supported. For a formal definition, please review the <u>Service Description</u>.

- **GetEmailAddress**
  Get the email address for the user

- **GetFirstName**
  Get the first name for the user

- **GetLastName**
  Get the last name for the user

- **GetLocation**
  Get the location id for the user

- **GetPhoneNumber**
  Get the phone number for the user

Figure 10-3. *.asmx file for the UserInformation service*

You can test any of the web methods by clicking on its name, for example, GetFirstName. When you do this, another page will ask you to provide a parameter. Provide your login name and click Invoke. This will open another window, and will show you an XML result that should include the name that was provided by the method, as shown in Figure 10-4.

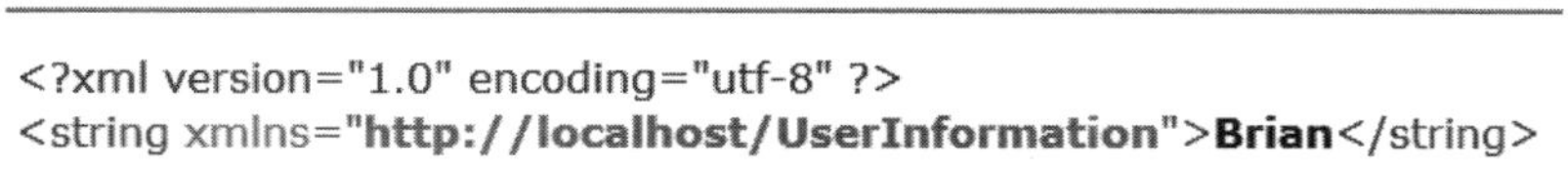

```
<?xml version="1.0" encoding="utf-8" ?>
<string xmlns="http://localhost/UserInformation">Brian</string>
```

Figure 10-4. *XML returned when GetFirstName invoked*

This result shows that the web service will be returning XML to the client that calls it. This also shows that the method is working correctly. To further test this, you can enter an invalid name in the UserLogin parameter and invoke the method again. If you do this, you should see an empty string in the XML results. Close the browser and the project.

Consuming a Web Service

Using a web service from a client application is called *consuming* the web service. This is done by first adding a web reference to the project and then using the exposed methods of the service.

Open the Help Desk web site you created previously. When the project appears, open the Solution Explorer and right-click the project name. Choose Add Web Reference from the menu. There are several ways to find the web service you want to reference. In the Add Web Reference window type **http://localhost/UserInformation/UserInformation.asmx** (using forward slashes) and click the Go button. VS will attempt to find the web service—if it does, the web methods available will appear, as shown in Figure 10-5.

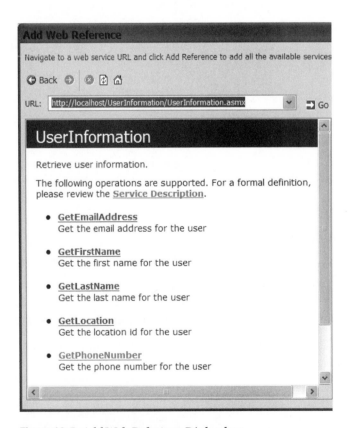

Figure 10-5. *Add Web Reference Dialog box*

Along with the displaying of the web methods, you can now also see a link called Service Description. This is the WSDL file that was discussed at the beginning of the chapter. If you click on the link you will see an XML file that describes the service.

Another way to find the web service is to search for all the web services on the local computer or on the local network. To test this out, click the Home button at the top of the Add Web Reference window (the Home button is the house icon). This will take you back to the original screen that appeared when you first attempted to add a web reference, as shown in Figure 10-6.

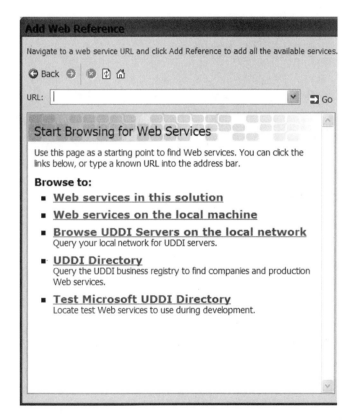

Figure 10-6. *Ways to find a web service*

Click the Web services on the local machine link. This will display a list of all of the web services on the local computer. Next, find the correct UserInformation web service and click that link. You should see the list of methods for the web service again. To add the web reference to the project, change the web reference name from localhost to UserInformation and then click the Add Reference button. You will now see a new folder within the project called App_Webreferences, with a folder inside it called UserInformation. The App_Webreferences folder contains all of the web references within the web site. The UserInformation folder contains all of the files necessary to work with the web service from within the web site. Notice the .wsdl file within this second folder.

Next, you need to use the web service. The best place to use this web service is within the AddTicket.aspx page. When the page is loaded, you'll determine the user's login, pass that to each method and then assign the results to the appropriate text box. If you remember from previously, the Session object already contains the user's login, so you don't need to determine that. Within the Page Load event add the following code:

```
Dim wsUserInformation As New UserInformation.UserInformation
```

This line of code will declare a variable to represent the web service. Next, add the following line of code to assign the value from the Session variable for the user login to the user login text box:

```
txtUserLogin.Text = Session("UserLogin").ToString
```

Now add one line for each control and method in order to call the web method and assign the returned value to the appropriate text box. The resulting code will be:

```
Dim wsUserInformation As New UserInformation.UserInformation
txtUserLogin.Text = Session("UserLogin").ToString
txtFirstName.Text =
wsUserInformation.GetFirstName(Session("UserLogin").ToString)
txtLastName.Text = wsUserInformation.GetLastName(Session("UserLogin").ToString)
txtPhoneNumber.Text = wsUserInformation.GetPhoneNumber
(Session("UserLogin").ToString)
txtEmailAddress.Text = wsUserInformation.GetEmailAddress

(Session("UserLogin").ToString)
```

To test this out, choose Start without debugging from the Debug menu. The AddTicket.aspx page will appear with all of the information filled in, as shown in Figure 10-7.

User Login	Brian
First Name	Brian
Last Name	Myers
Phone Number	555-5555
Location	Select a Location
Email Address	email@company.com

Figure 10-7. *Data is displayed.*

The location assignment was left out of the previous code because it's a little different. You need to make the drop-down list use the value from the web service. To do this, add the following lines of code to the page load event after the call to AddItem:

```
Dim intLocation As Integer
intLocation = wsUserInformation.GetLocation(Session("userlogin").ToString)
If intLocation > 0 Then
DDLocation.SelectedValue =
DDLocation.Items.FindByValue(intLocation.ToString).Value
Else
DDLocation.SelectedValue = "999"
End If
```

The first line declares a holding variable, which is used on the second line to receive the value from the web method. The third line determines whether the value from the web method was greater than 0. The fourth line selects the value from the drop-down list, (found by using the FindByValue method of the items collection within the drop-down list). The FindByValue method requires a parameter telling it which value to find. Basically the FindByValue method tries to find a value within the collection and then provide its value. If the value from the web method isn't greater than 0 then the Select a location item is selected.

To test what happens when the login is not found, open the Global.asax page and change the Session assignment to `Session.Add("UserLogin", strName & "1")`. This is an easy way to test what happens if the user login is not a value and it's easy to reverse. Now, choose Start without debugging from the Debug menu. No information (other than the login name) will appear, since the login name now has a 1 attached to the end and is therefore invalid.

Conclusion

In this chapter, I introduced the concepts behind web services and expanded the Help Desk application by creating a web service. I showed you how to use this web service to provide user information and how to consume that web service within the Help Desk application.

Index

forums.apress.com

FOR PROFESSIONALS BY PROFESSIONALS™

JOIN THE APRESS FORUMS AND BE PART OF OUR COMMUNITY. You'll find discussions that cover topics of interest to IT professionals, programmers, and enthusiasts just like you. If you post a query to one of our forums, you can expect that some of the best minds in the business—especially Apress authors, who all write with *The Expert's Voice™*—will chime in to help you. Why not aim to become one of our most valuable participants (MVPs) and win cool stuff? Here's a sampling of what you'll find:

DATABASES

Data drives everything.

Share information, exchange ideas, and discuss any database programming or administration issues.

INTERNET TECHNOLOGIES AND NETWORKING

Try living without plumbing (and eventually IPv6).

Talk about networking topics including protocols, design, administration, wireless, wired, storage, backup, certifications, trends, and new technologies.

JAVA

We've come a long way from the old Oak tree.

Hang out and discuss Java in whatever flavor you choose: J2SE, J2EE, J2ME, Jakarta, and so on.

MAC OS X

All about the Zen of OS X.

OS X is both the present and the future for Mac apps. Make suggestions, offer up ideas, or boast about your new hardware.

OPEN SOURCE

Source code is good; understanding (open) source is better.

Discuss open source technologies and related topics such as PHP, MySQL, Linux, Perl, Apache, Python, and more.

PROGRAMMING/BUSINESS

Unfortunately, it is.

Talk about the Apress line of books that cover software methodology, best practices, and how programmers interact with the "suits."

WEB DEVELOPMENT/DESIGN

Ugly doesn't cut it anymore, and CGI is absurd.

Help is in sight for your site. Find design solutions for your projects and get ideas for building an interactive Web site.

SECURITY

Lots of bad guys out there—the good guys need help.

Discuss computer and network security issues here. Just don't let anyone else know the answers!

TECHNOLOGY IN ACTION

Cool things. Fun things.

It's after hours. It's time to play. Whether you're into LEGO® MINDSTORMS™ or turning an old PC into a DVR, this is where technology turns into fun.

WINDOWS

No defenestration here.

Ask questions about all aspects of Windows programming, get help on Microsoft technologies covered in Apress books, or provide feedback on any Apress Windows book.

HOW TO PARTICIPATE:

Go to the Apress Forums site at **http://forums.apress.com/**.

Click the New User link.